Adventures In Church Growth

Nothing done
for eternity so are
cars take our rest
my folks have bought at least
2 - 3 cars + each was to be their last one
now they need another

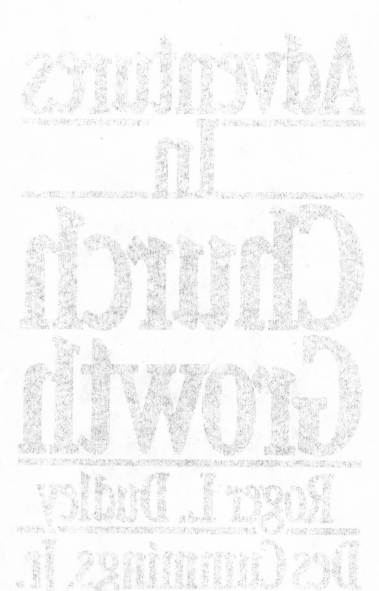

Adventures In Church Growth

Roger L. Dudley

Des Cummings, Jr.

Adventures In Church Growth

Roger L. Dudley
Des Cummings, Jr.

Review and Herald Publishing Association
Washington, DC 20039-0555
Hagerstown, MD 21740

Copyright © 1983 by
Review and Herald Publishing Association

This book was
Edited by Gerald Wheeler
Designed by Richard Steadham
Type set: 11/12 Baskerville

Library of Congress Cataloging in Publication Data
Dudley, Roger L.
    Adventures in church growth.

    1. Church growth—Seventh-day Adventists. 2. Seventh-day Adventists—Doctrines. I. Cummings, Des., Jr. II. Title.
BV652.25.D83   1983   254'.5   83-16089
ISBN 0-8280-0228-2

PRINTED IN U.S.A.

Acknowledgments

During the time that we have been conducting research on the subject of church growth, we have been blessed with the assistance of several able Seminary students. While many people have contributed, we would especially thank Peter Bath, Greg Clark, Gary Fogelquist, and Don Ritterskamp for their substantial aid. Lorena Bidwell engineered most of our computer programming.

We are grateful to Robert L. Dale, of the North American Division office, for his encouragement and suggestions, and to Charles E. Bradford, who made available a generous research grant.

Much appreciation goes to Marquita Rand, who typed the final manuscript.

Finally, we would like to honor our wives, Peggy and Mary Lou, whose supportive understanding provided inspiration for the project, and Des's children Derek and Tracy, whose faith and prayers have served as a source of encouragement.

Roger L. Dudley and Des Cummings, Jr.

Contents

Introduction 9

What Is Growth? 13

Focus—Not Hocus-pocus 23

More Than a Numbers Game 31

A Message From Kelley 41

The Adventist Church: Three Distinctive Experiences 51

Owning Goals 59

A Model for Church Planning 67

Knowing Your Own Community 79

Making the Most of a Profile 91

Mobilizing the Members 109

Whom Are We Winning? 119

The Ogre of Apostasy 135

The Church's Agenda in the Coming Decade 151

Introduction

In November of 1979 we received an exciting challenge. The Andrews University board of trustees authorized the establishment of the Institute of Church Ministry (ICM) as a branch of the Theological Seminary and invited us to direct the new enterprise.

ICM represented a new concept in ministry. It brought the resources of the university (such as trained personnel, comprehensive media centers, and giant computer facilities) to the service of the Seventh-day Adventist Church in its mission to the world. ICM operates by performing surveys and other research studies, compiling demographic profiles of major cities, conducting continuing-education experiences, preparing curricular materials, operating a telephone ministry, assembling resource materials, and consulting with pastors and administrators.

Much of our work has centered upon the field of church growth. Our first project involved a study of it in the North American Division. We surveyed 250 pastors of churches randomly selected from the entire division. In 193 of the churches we also surveyed the members present at a Sabbath worship service. Altogether we collected more than 8,200 member questionnaires—the largest data bank on church growth ever assembled on Seventh-day Adventists. The publication of the results in the prestigious scholarly journal *Review of Religious Research* (June, 1983) affirmed the validity of the research.

Since that first study, ICM has conducted church growth research for a number of conferences, including Washington, Texas, Georgia-Cumberland, Hawaiian, Illinois, Oregon, Rocky Mountain, Northern California, and Ohio. Such studies have added thousands of members to our data banks and have contributed much to our knowledge about how church growth takes place in the Adventist Church.

They not only described member and pastor attitudes and practices but correlated them with the actual and kingdom (soon to be explained) growth rates of the individual churches. Thus it is possible to see what characteristics growing churches exhibit, and, contrariwise, the traits of declining ones. In addition to empirical fieldwork, we carefully reviewed and digested the most relevant literature in the area of church growth.

Both sources form the basis for this book. We might have called it "What We Have Learned About Church Growth" or "Adventist Church Growth in the Light of Recent Research." At any rate, we felt that it was time that ICM shared its learnings with the church in a broader way, especially in view of the mighty surge of Faith Action Advance in North America.

While we were in the process of writing this book, two other exciting developments took place. The first involved the preparation of a new set of guidelines by the North American Division called "Dynamics of Church Growth." It outlined a strategy for the division, using the four basic steps of planning, equipping, implementing, and evaluating. The program emphasizes the local church as the primary unit for growth. Every other branch of the denomination must support the local congregation.

The second development was the adoption of "The Caring Church" concept. The growing church is the caring

INTRODUCTION

church—the one that finds and meets the needs of the people around it. As we studied "Dynamics of Church Growth" and "The Caring Church," we were thrilled to find how completely our research supported their concepts. Indeed, our work seems but an expansion and an illustration of their principles. We believe that God has led in helping us to prepare this book just at this challenging hour.

Who will read this book? We hope that it will prove valuable to denominational leaders, pastors, and lay members serious about the mission of their church. How can one best use this book? We see it as a study manual that the church will employ in reorganizing itself for service. In a prayer meeting series or other appropriate group setting, the church may carefully study and seek to implement the principles and strategies described.

We wish to acknowledge frankly that scientific research can never substitute for the Holy Spirit. Without His power working in the church, real growth can never take place. And yet God does not send the Holy Spirit to sanction ignorance. As we do our best to discover and cooperate with the laws of human behavior, the Spirit can best bless our efforts and lead the church into that period of unprecedented growth known as the latter rain. As we have pursued our work, we have faithfully tried to follow the motto that "knowledge is power only when united with true piety." *

Roger L. Dudley and Des Cummings, Jr.

Reference
* Ellen G. White, *Testimonies to Ministers* (Mountain View, Calif.: Pacific Press Pub. Assn., 1944), p. 197.

1

What Is Growth?

Trees grow. Puppies grow. Babies grow. Relationships grow. If they are healthy and normal, that is. So do churches. Growth is an essential property of life. When living things cease to grow, they begin to deteriorate. So every Christian is for church growth. Well, not quite.

The "church growth movement" has drawn serious criticism from certain sections of the Christian community in recent years. Even among Seventh-day Adventists, an emphasis on numerical increase has caused some ministers and laity to have an uneasy feeling. Why? How could any dedicated Christian possibly have anything but the greatest excitement about the prospects of a growing church?

The Case Against Growth

One reason for a lack of enthusiasm for filling the pews is the belief that the church simply cannot assimilate large numbers of new members without scrimping on the careful preparation time needed by each one. "We can grow rapidly only at the expense of padding our membership rolls with those who are poorly grounded in the fundamentals of

Christian belief and practice," the argument runs. "We do not wish to sacrifice quality for quantity." It is a legitimate point that church growth planners must consider.

A second reason, one held by many mainline scholars, is that church growth does not primarily fall under the control of the church; outside, "contextual" factors (as opposed to "institutional" factors—those under the control of the church) largely determine what is happening. For example, Dean Hoge reports a study in which he shows that the three contextual factors of family income, percent living in the West, and number of children in the family can explain more than half the total variance in denominational growth rates between 1965 and 1975 if one enters them into the regression equation (the statistical method used) first.[1] Therefore, why put a heavy priority on growth and thus burden churches with guilt when actually they are largely the victims of the environments in which they find themselves?

Of course, such a position does have some validity. Some settings are much more conducive to growth than others, and some communities may have little receptivity to the gospel message for one reason or another. However, within contextual limits each church must decide what it will do with the mission field assigned to it. Also, we should point out that one obtains Hoge's conclusions by entering the contextual factors into the regression equation first. This is based upon his assumption that contextual factors are causally prior to those institutional factors over which the church does have control. But the assumption is debatable. If one enters the institutional factors into his study first, they account for nearly *all* the variance in the growth rates.

At any rate, we would not wish our emphasis on church growth to put a "guilt trip" on congregations that find themselves in unfortunate circumstances. Enough guilt already exists without our adding to it. The thesis of this book is not that every church ought to grow at the same rate, but that by using the principles we will present, every church can maximize its own potential for growth, given the community in which it finds itself.

Theologian Robert Evans has persuasively presented the

third argument.[2] He holds that the church has a primary mission to the larger society. It is to be the voice of conscience, challenging and transforming the contemporary culture—a role historically assumed by mainline Protestantism. While this does not mean that churches will not or should not add new converts, a preoccupation with its own growth may be a selfish neglect of its responsibility to society at large. Thus Evans writes, "Numerical church growth is important but not primary to the transformation of the church and the culture."

The church must be faithful to its calling above everything else, and under this model, faithfulness may require taking public positions that will limit growth possibilities. "What God requires of the church is not growth but faithfulness." "The expectation of faithfulness is to share, not necessarily to succeed." We could certainly agree with some of these thoughts if one does not use them as a rationalization for failure or a cop-out for doing nothing. Evans himself believes that the church must find a balance between faithfulness and effectiveness.

While the first three reasons have all been somewhat rational and deserve serious consideration, the final argument that we will present has more of an emotional basis. In fact, few will state it openly. But it is there nevertheless. Some small congregations feel threatened by the possibility of an influx of new members. They dread loss of their positions of influence and control. Even more, they worry that the atmosphere and style of the church will change. Comfortable with their group and the way they have been doing things for many years, they don't want the transformations that they perceive will come if a majority of another generation or culture takes charge. Like the early Jewish Christians, they desire to control carefully the entry of Gentiles into the church.[3] We must be sensitive to such feelings as we patiently educate those who hold them to see that God's will for them and their congregation may well call for some personal sacrifice.

Internal and External Growth

These questions finally focus on whether churches should

emphasize internal spiritual growth or external numerical growth. Fortunately this is not a true dichotomy. The Bible tells us to "grow in the grace and knowledge of our Lord and Savior Jesus Christ" (2 Peter 3:18). It also states that the purpose of spiritual gifts is that "the body of Christ may be built up until we all reach unity in the faith and in the knowledge of the Son of God and become mature, attaining to the whole measure of the fullness of Christ" (Eph. 4:12, 13). And Ellen White has written, "When the character of Christ shall be perfectly reproduced in His people, then He will come to claim them as His own."[4] Certainly growth in Christlikeness and spiritual maturity must ever be an important goal of the church.

On the other hand, the New Testament church also increased numerically. Under the influence of the Holy Spirit and the Pentecost experience, "the Lord added to their number daily those who were being saved" (Acts 2:47; see also verse 41; chaps. 5:14; 6:1, 7). We do not have to accept an either-or situation. Numerical expansion and spiritual nurture do not oppose each other. They are both necessary components of the same process—establishing the kingdom of God. Neither will be done without the other.

Churches will not grow numerically unless their members are nurtured in spiritual growth, preserved from apostasy, and incorporated as responsible members of the body of Christ who will gladly share their faith. Churches will not grow spiritually unless they have a constant supply of new converts to provide a fresh infusion of spiritual life and unless the renewed members have outlets for service. Which is more important, internal or external growth? We might as well ask the same question of breathing in or breathing out. You can't have one without the other for long. So it is with internal and external growth in the church.

Of course, a pastor could give his energies for a while merely to baptizing people and forget about everything else. In a mad rush to beat the statistics game, he could decide that the only thing that really mattered was "get them in the tank." But this would soon prove counterproductive. The church growth we talk about in this book does not at all mean baptizing anybody you can find and then moving on to new conquests. It involves confronting lost humans with the claims of Jesus Christ, leading them to a decision, nurturing their spiritual growth, assimilating them as responsible members of the church body, and inspiring them to spend the rest of their lives sharing their new-found faith with others as they become God's co-workers in the establishment of His kingdom on earth. So we will not neglect spiritual growth in this book. But at the same time we wish every responsive person to hear Christ's final message and to rejoice in the fellowship of His church. We long to see the walls of meetinghouses bulging out as men and women, young and old, press into the fellowship of His kingdom.

The Unique Mission of the Church

Seventh-day Adventists believe that their organization is not just another church with a different day of worship than the majority of the Christian churches, but a special movement God raised up during the last years of earth's history to prepare people everywhere for the coming of Jesus and citizenship in the new and perfect world.

Our unique mission calls for the proclamation of the gospel to every nation, kindred, tongue, and people (Matt. 24:14; Rev. 5:9) in the special setting of the messages of the three angels of Revelation 14. But it requires more than mere proclamation. We are to lead people out of the world and the churches that have fallen into error (Rev. 18:1-4), and into God's remnant church (chap. 12:17). Then we are to baptize and make them into disciples (Matt. 28:18-20). If the church is faithful to its commission, both individual congregations and the church at large will increase in size as people hear and heed the summons to join this heaven-bound movement. They will also grow in spiritual dimensions as members more and more come to reflect the likeness of Jesus (1 John 3:2; Eph. 4:15, 16).

Ways to Grow

In attempting to understand church growth, we need to separate the various streams that serve as its sources of supply.

We may classify them under three headings:

1. *Transfer growth* takes place as people who already hold membership in another church within the denomination move their membership to the roll of a particular congregation. Especially if it occurs in an area where members have several options, transfer growth may say something about the ability of a congregation to minister to peoples' various needs and therefore can be a valuable indicator. However, it does not result in the unchurched becoming part of the body of Christ. Therefore, a church that experiences rapid growth but finds it to be nearly all of the transfer type should not rest on its self-congratulatory laurels.

2. *Biological growth* results from taking into membership those young people reared in the home of believers and nurtured within the church's day and/or Sabbath school educational system. Some students of church growth estimate that biological increase will average around 25 percent per decade even if no other growth occurs.

3. *Conversion growth* is bringing into the congregation people who are not transferring from another church and who are not sons and daughters of present members. Only it will expand the kingdom of God beyond its present boundaries. It alone measures our impact upon the world.

In saying this we are not discounting the importance of biological growth nor are we saying that young people who join the church are not converted. Both of us have spent a major portion of our professional lives in youth ministry, and we place a high priority upon the evangelism and holding of our young people. Neither are we suggesting that we can take such baptisms for granted. Failing to win far too many of our own youth, we should be constantly studying how to reach, hold, and train every one. Personally we have dedicated ourselves to that task. On the other hand, we must recognize that if most of our baptisms come from biological growth, we are not speaking Christ's message to the community around us. While we must save our own, we must also reach out to others—those who will not hear God's Word without us. To this end it is helpful to analyze our baptisms as to biological and conversion growth even though the denomination does not keep such statistics at present.

But, of course, growth is not merely evangelizing people. You could bring in a large number in a year and still show a loss if the back door stands wide open. The church can suffer church decline in three ways:

1. *Transfer loss.* Members move away and send for their letters. Economic conditions may force members to leave the community and seek work elsewhere. Students may go away to academy or college in pursuit of a Christian education. A group may transfer out to spawn a new congregation as a mission project. But whenever considerable transfer loss occurs, the church should carefully analyze the problem to determine the reasons behind it. Perhaps the congregation is failing to meet the spiritual needs of some of its members and should restudy its scope of ministries.

2. *Death.* This is out of the control of the church (except as we emphasize the message of healthful living). A specially significant source of loss in older congregations, it is one reason why churches with a larger proportion of young people are more likely to be growing ones.

3. *Apostasy loss.* This is the most tragic of all. People who once made a commitment to Jesus Christ give up their faith. Heavy apostasy (sometimes called reversion) limits church growth, but it involves more than a matter of statistics. Each case represents a valuable human being turning from life to death. We must do most careful study and pray often to prevent this (Matt. 24:13; 2 Peter 3:17). In a later chapter we will deal with some research findings on this subject. Under apostasy loss we also include those who are no longer in touch with the church and who cannot be located to assess their spiritual experience, and so are termed "missing" and dropped.

Actual and Kingdom Growth

We use two measures to compute growth rates. *Actual* growth rate is defined as subtracting the membership at the beginning of the period under study from the membership at the close and expressing the difference as a percentage of the beginning membership. *Kingdom* growth rate involves subtracting the number dropped for apostasy (and missing) during the period from the number added by baptism (and profession of faith) and stating the difference as a percentage of the beginning membership.

Thus, while actual growth looks at all methods that affect membership figures, kingdom growth ignores transfers to and from other Adventist churches and loss by death and deals directly with the conversion-apostasy ratio. Kingdom growth is the sum of both biological and conversion growth. While we would recommend calculating these components of kingdom growth separately for your church, we could not do this in our research because official statistics of the denomination do not provide such information.

To grasp the difference between actual and kingdom growth better, consider the Adventist Church in Typical City:

Membership on January 1	=	100 members
Add during year		
by baptism		10
by profession of faith		1
by transfer in		12
Total added		23
Drop during year		
by transfer out		5
by death		3
by apostasy		5
by missing		1
Total dropped		14
Membership on December 31	=	109 members

With these figures in hand we can easily calculate our growth rates:

Actual growth = closing membership minus opening membership divided by beginning membership or

$$\frac{109 - 100}{100} = .09 \text{ or } 9\%$$

Kingdom growth = baptisms + professions minus apostasies + missing divided by beginning membership or

$$\frac{(10 + 1) - (5 + 1)}{100} = .05 \text{ or } 5\%$$

WHAT IS GROWTH?

We will often refer to these statistics as we report various research findings in this book.

Church growth then has both an internal spiritual and an external numerical quality. Both go together, and both are absolutely essential to the fulfillment of the Great Commission. This book is dedicated to the task of helping the pastor and church member to make a success of both under the blessing of God.

References

[1] Dean R. Hoge, "A Test of Theories of Denominational Growth and Decline," in Dean R. Hoge and David A. Roozen, eds., *Understanding Church Growth and Decline: 1950-1978* (New York: Pilgrim Press, 1979), pp. 179-197.

[2] Robert A. Evans, "Recovering the Church's Transforming Middle: Theological Reflections on the Balance Between Faithfulness and Effectiveness," in *ibid.*, pp. 288-314.

[3] For further expansion of this theme, see Carl S. Dudley, *Making the Small Church Effective* (Nashville, Tenn.: Abingdon Press, 1978).

[4] Ellen G. White, *Christ's Object Lessons* (Washington, D.C.: Review and Herald Pub. Assn., 1941), p. 69.

2

Focus—Not Hocus-pocus

When you were young, did you ever play with a magnifying glass? Wasn't it fun to catch the rays of the sun and concentrate them into one tiny, yet powerful, spot of light? Play that little beam on a piece of paper, and you could see a wisp of smoke begin to curl up. A few seconds later the paper darkened to a brown hue and soon burst into flames. Even as a child you were learning something about the power unleased when you focus energy.

The same principle applies to church growth. In our study of church growth in the North American Division, we asked the pastors of 250 churches this question: To what extent is every phase of church activity focused on church growth? Pastors could respond on a scale of one to five, ranging from "each phase independent" to "every phase focused on growth." Of the sixty-eight items on the questionnaire, this item had the strongest correlation with actual growth and the second strongest with kingdom growth.[1] We found the question also to be strongly related to growth in studies among Adventist pastors in Hawaii and in Atlanta, Georgia.[2]

The members see it that way also. Our division-wide study

collected data from 8,211 members attending 193 churches. We asked them to rate their churches on a five-point continuum from "not a soul-winning church" to "soul-winning church." Those ratings had the highest correlations with both actual and kingdom growth of any questions on the survey. The relationship between members perceiving their churches as soul-winning and the growth of those churches was the strongest one we found in the study. The same item acted as a significant predictor of growth in the Hawaiian and Atlanta studies and also among Adventist churches in Texas and the State of Washington.[3]

Another question on the survey requested the members to rate the emphasis that their pastor placed on soul winning. Evaluations ranged from "little importance" to "top priority." Significant relationships occurred between this item and both actual and kingdom growth on the national study and also in the Atlanta area.

So the evidence seems clear. The church that makes growth the top-priority item and focuses every area of church life to this end is the one that grows. Growth does not occur by accident. Neither does it happen by magic—a sort of hocus-pocus. Rather the key word is *focus*. The pastor and the congregation who learn this lesson and put it into practice are, under the blessing of God, on their way to great exploits for their Lord.

The Cost of Growth

But wait! It's not quite as easy and as simple as it sounds. In fact, it is quite difficult and costly. Peter Wagner has written, "The indispensable condition for a growing church is that it wants to grow and is willing to pay the price for growth."[4]

Could it really be that a congregation and/or its pastor might not desire growth? Yes, although the congregation is more likely to hold such attitudes subconsciously than to state them openly. The first chapter treated this theme in some detail. By way of summary, we may note three reasons for growth-reluctant churches:

1. The attitude that if the church is faithful to its high standards it will remain small. Most people choose to follow

the broad downward path rather than the strait and narrow way. Therefore, any large influx of converts must indicate that the church has compromised its distinctiveness. God will save only a small remnant.

2. The feeling of comfortableness in a group where everyone knows everyone else may vanish. Many congregations of few members have been together for years and have that "family feeling." To let in a lot of strangers might change the dynamics and destroy a primary support group.

3. The threat of loss of control by those who have long served as "pillars" in the congregation may cause resistance to growth. The old-timers sense that the power base may well shift as the newcomers begin to outnumber them.

And what about the price? It will call for time, for energy, for money, and for the willingness to sacrifice the familiar and accustomed ways of doing things. Further, it will demand the setting of goals and the taking of risks. And above all, it will necessitate a reevaluation and a new ordering of priorities.

The 1976 Annual Council of the Seventh-day Adventist Church issued a stirring challenge in a document entitled "Evangelism and Finishing God's Work." [5] We may sum up the theme of this historic statement as: "It is for us now to determine the steps to take in order to give absolute priority to evangelism at all levels and on all fronts." In the light of this, the Council voted that "every effort be made to bring about a clear, unequivocal, churchwide understanding of the crucial nature and primacy of evangelism."

Further on, the document attempts to clarify the role of the pastor by quoting from *Gospel Workers*, p. 16: "The minister who is a co-worker with Christ will have a deep sense of the sacredness of his work. . . . He has but one object in view—the saving of the lost." [6] The statement also called upon the "Church Evangelism Council [in some churches the church board functions as the evangelism council] in each church . . . to fulfill its potential as the 'command center' to organize every member and the whole church for one-to-one witnessing and all-out evangelism." Indeed, the entire 1976 Annual Council action deserves careful and frequent study as church leaders and local congregations struggle to learn how to focus all their efforts on bringing about responsible church growth.

"Wants to grow and is willing to pay the price." The cost may be high indeed, but the growth we gain will be well worth it, for it comes in obedience to our Lord's command. We will have the satisfaction of knowing that increasing numbers of lost men and women, boys and girls, are hearing and accepting the good news of His salvation.

Both the Word and the research have taught us that growing churches focus on growth. They tailor every individual activity to evangelism. While the church may (and should) have a variety of ministries, each exists only as it has a rationale in the overall plan of evangelism. Donald McGavran calls this "seeing everything through church-growth eyes."

Obviously, both pastor and members will have to want their church to grow—want it with all their hearts—to make it happen. And they will have to plan for it. Robert Schuller, who built the Garden Grove Community Church in California from a tiny handful into one of the greatest congregations in America, has said, "If you fail to plan, you plan to fail." [7] The church that takes the Great Commission seriously will be willing to pay the price for growth and count it cheap enough.

Is This Church Lopsided?

Does the church that focuses on growth become unbalanced? Does it forget about Christian education, nurture of the members' spiritual life, health programs, marriage and family enrichment, and other body-building ministries? NO! NO! NO! As a matter of fact, it will probably have more such activities than the stagnating one. A number of our research studies have shown that churches with a more complete ministry for all age groups are more likely to be growing congregations than are those with limited ministries.

It is important to remind ourselves continually that merely baptizing people is not the same as church growth. While the practice may result in a temporary "shot in the arm," it quickly proves counterproductive and self-defeating. Church growth must also involve incorporating the new converts into responsible church membership and equipping them for further service. It concerns itself as much with quality as with quantity.

It is a false dichotomy to set evangelism above body-building ministries. Both are absolutely essential. Remember the question we posed earlier: Which is more important, breathing in or breathing out? After all, a wider variety of services will attract more new people, and members are less likely to drop out of a church that is meeting their needs.

So it is not growth *or* stop-smoking plans, marriage and family enrichment, diet and nutrition programs, stress control clinics, et cetera. Rather it is evangelism *through* such ministries that constitutes the focused church. It is not outreach *versus* nurture, but rather nurture to make outreach possible and to mature the spiritual lives of the new believers.

The Caring Church, then, has a multitude of ministries. But they do not exist as so many separate entities, each spinning off in its own orbit. They all focus on growth. The church demands that every program demonstrate how it will help the congregation grow. For example, it does not conduct health programs for the purpose of making "healthy sinners," but that in compassion the church may meet the felt needs of suffering fellow humans and open the way for them to find complete healing of the whole man.

Recognizing the power generated by focusing, the 1976 Annual Council called for "positive leadership through departmental expertise . . . to provide the necessary diversity of redemptive programs and materials that can be used to organize, inspire, train, equip, and lead our vast army of church members into programs that are pre-evangelistic, evangelistic, and post-evangelistic in nature, and which will definitely reach souls for Christ and truth."[8]

Perhaps it would be helpful to select one nurturing ministry and examine it in further detail to discover how the church could focus it on church growth. It may serve as an example of how to view all such programs. Since one of us teaches in the field of marriage and family, that may serve as a good illustration.

Certainly the abundance of family problems and the state of marriage in society at large point to the need for such a healing ministry. The Adventist home is not exempt from such difficulties either, and the church has begun to take seriously the building of Christian families as attested to by the creation of the Home and Family Service in the General Conference in 1975. Since then the denomination has developed a number of resources and programs to meet the pressing problems. Some have felt that such a program constitutes a detour on the road to evangelizing the world, a squandering of resources that the church could better use in direct evangelism. Yet, properly focused, marriage and family programs are a complement to the church's mission for at least three reasons:

1. Unless we have happy Christian homes, we will not have a strong base from which to reach out to the world. People who live in a constant atmosphere of quarreling, misunderstanding, or strained silence usually find themselves emotionally drained and depressed. They do not have the vibrancy to go out and share the gospel in a way that gives it personal relevance. While they may be able to argue the doctrines, they can't share the testimony of "what God has done for me."

2. The world will find itself attracted to the church not only, or even primarily, because the message is true, but because it offers a more satisfying life. If the church can offer love, joy, peace, and fulfillment where only hatred, misery, strife, and emptiness have existed, humanity will listen and respond. When Jesus said, " 'All men will know that you are my disciples if you love one another' " (John 13:35), did He not include the relationships within families as well as between them? But if the world sees that as much unhappiness, division, and divorce exist among the families of the church as among those of the world, will it not conclude that our message is only "head" religion?

3. Marriage and family programs have direct evangelistic potential. We are constantly seeking ways to gain a hearing for our message. A generation or two ago evangelists approached the public with a series of prophecy lectures beginning with Daniel 2. In most places that method will not earn a hearing today. We must seek entering wedges that will meet the felt

needs of the communities we serve. The health emphasis (stop-smoking plans, weight control, cooking schools) has proved to be one effective approach. Marriage and family programs have great potential to be equally or even more effective. People want to know how to make their marriage work and how to parent their children. The Caring Church could earn a hearing with such programs that would open the way for people to consider the further beauties of Seventh-day Adventist teachings.

Special Assignment for Your Church Evangelism Council. List all the programs and ministries in which your church presently engages. Then next to each item on the list, write as many ways as you can think of that could make that particular item contribute to church growth. If you can't find any way, reevaluate the reason for its existence.

A Work of Faith

Peter Wagner expands his previous statement just a bit: "The indispensable condition for a growing church is that it wants to grow. . . . Wanting to grow and planning for growth is another way of applying Biblical faith." [9] As the church focuses, it must believe that God will bless its efforts with success. "Without faith it is impossible to please God, because anyone who comes to him must believe that . . . he rewards those who earnestly seek him" (Heb. 11:6). " 'If you have faith as small as a mustard seed, you can say to this mountain, "Move from here to there" and it will move. Nothing will be impossible for you' " (Matt. 17:20).

Ellen White has encouraged us that "when we give ourselves wholly to God and in our work follow His directions, He makes Himself responsible for its accomplishment. He would not have us conjecture as to the success of our honest endeavors. Not once should we even think of failure. We are to cooperate with One who knows no failure." [10]

In our study of church growth in the North American Division, we asked the pastors to rate the potential of the local church for real growth on a five-point continuum from "no potential" to "unlimited potential." We found that the high ratings significantly related to both actual and kingdom growth. And we discovered a similar correlation in Atlanta, Washington, and Texas.

Church growth is an adventure in faith. Simply put, we cannot accomplish anything worthwhile unless we believe that we can. Robert Schuller, who preaches to thousands each week at the Garden Grove Community Church, has well articulated the concept of "possibility thinking." He began to set growth-stimulating goals when he noticed a slogan on a calendar that said, "I'd rather attempt to do something great and fail than attempt to do nothing and succeed." Schuller says, "You've got to believe it to see it." [11]

The Adventist pastor who leads a growing congregation is also a possibility thinker. He believes in the potential of his church to grow, that nothing can stop it from growing. Eager anticipation also fills the members. They have a sense of camaraderie, a sort of team spirit infused with faith—"The Lord is working with us! We are in partnership with Him! Our church is serious about fulfilling the divine commission." When the members sense that their church exists for the purpose of bringing people to Christ, things begin to happen.

So there it is! A church that wishes to grow must plan to grow and pay the price. This suggests a purposeful, intentional ministry—a focusing of the energies and resources of the congregation on top priorities.

References
[1] Roger L. Dudley and Des Cummings, Jr., "A Study of Factors Relating to Church Growth in the North American Division of Seventh-day Adventists" (Berrien Springs, Mich.: Institute of Church Ministry, Andrews University, 1981).
[2] Greg Clark, Roger L. Dudley, and Des Cummings, Jr., "A Study of Factors Relating to Church Growth in the Hawaiian Mission of Seventh-day Adventists" (Berrien Springs, Mich.: Institute of Church Ministry, Andrews University, 1981), and "A Study of Factors Relating to Church Growth in the Greater Atlanta Area" (Berrien Springs, Mich.: Institute of Church Ministry, Andrews University, 1981).
[3] ————, "A Study of Factors Relating to Church Growth and Apostasy in the Texas Conference of Seventh-day Adventists" (Berrien Springs, Mich.: Institute of Church Ministry, Andrews University, 1981); Roger L. Dudley, Des Cummings, Jr., Mary Lou Cummings, and Greg Clark, "A Study of Factors Relating to Church Growth and Apostasy in the Washington Conference of Seventh-day Adventists" (Berrien Springs, Mich.: Institute of Church Ministry, Andrews University, 1981).
[4] C. Peter Wagner, *Your Church Can Grow* (Glendale, Calif.: Regal Books, 1976), p. 49.
[5] Annual Council of Seventh-day Adventists, "Evangelism and Finishing God's Work," *Ministry*, vol. 49 (December, 1976), pp. 3-10.
[6] Ellen G. White, *Gospel Workers* (Washington, D.C.: Review & Herald Pub. Assn., 1948), p. 16.
[7] Quoted in Wagner, *op. cit.*, pp. 49, 50.
[8] Annual Council, *op. cit.*, p. 9.
[9] Wagner, *op. cit.*, p. 47.
[10] Ellen G. White, *Christ's Object Lessons*, p. 363.
[11] Quoted in Wagner, *op. cit.*, p. 53. See also Robert H. Schuller, *Your Church Has Real Possibilities* (Glendale, Calif.: Regal Books, 1974).

3

More Than a Numbers Game

Frankly, some pastors and lay leaders experience a degree of fear when the talk turns to church growth. They become somewhat uncomfortable when conference officials begin to strongly promote finishing God's mission and suggest that every church ought to be in there doing its part. Perhaps it is because too many have misunderstood the subject.

Local leaders may feel that the whole growth idea is a pressure program to add numbers and that it comes down from a group of executives who have nothing else to do but to think up new jobs for already-overburdened ministers. In a later chapter we'll talk about how and where the church sets its goals and programs. At this point, however, let's look at the "numbers game."

Church growth is not a desperate attempt to baptize people—anybody—just so the pastor can make his record look good. Pastors who get caught up in that turbulent stream may find themselves baptizing ever-younger children, individuals who have not demonstrated any signs of conversion, and those with low sales resistance. They may neglect their present flock and forget about newly baptized converts as they rush off to fresh conquests.

Such pastors sacrifice their own initial ideals and prostitute their ministry. Playing the "numbers game" may produce a temporary spurt in the statistics, but the seeming success is short-lived. It will not result in healthy long-term church growth. Let's see why.

Internal Spiritual Growth

Church growth refers not merely to an outer measurable expansion, but also to an inner experience within the body of Christ. "But grow in the grace and knowledge of our Lord and Savior Jesus Christ" (2 Peter 3:18), the apostle admonishes. And Scripture further tells us that "we know that when he appears, we shall be like him. . . . Everyone who has this hope in him purifies himself, just as he is pure" (1 John 3:2, 3).

To be faithful to our calling means that each individual member of the church will spend a lifetime growing to be more like Jesus. And as the maturing experience takes place in each life, the congregation as a whole becomes more representative of the love of our wonderful God. An onlooking world can increasingly discern the body of Christ in this band of believers.

Church growth must involve all of this. Its insistence on quality balances its concern for quantity. The whole includes proclaiming the gospel, winning and baptizing converts, incorporating them into responsible membership, nurturing their spiritual development, equipping them for further service, motivating them to missionary tasks, and supporting them as they go out to exercise their gifts in bringing in still others. Unless the whole cycle is in place and functioning, the feverish attempt to add to the membership rolls by baptizing will soon break down for lack of a support system. At least three reasons indicate why this is so:

1. *Real numerical growth comes by the blessing of God.* In His final instructions Jesus told His followers, " 'You will receive power when the Holy Spirit comes on you; and you will be my witnesses in Jerusalem, and in all Judea and Samaria, and to the ends of the earth" (Acts 1:8). The extraordinary events on the day of Pentecost and the rapid numerical growth pictured

in the early chapters of Acts occurred only through a special outpouring of the Holy Spirit. And the Lord cannot bestow such blessing on the congregation that is not experiencing inner spiritual growth.

> The Lord does not now work to bring many souls into the truth, because of the church members who have never been converted and those who were once converted but who have backslidden. What influence would these unconsecrated members have on new converts? Would they not make of no effect the God-given message which His people are to bear?[1]

2. *Our message to the world involves an inner experience.* Unless they are growing in their relationship with Jesus, church members will have no motivation to reach out to their communities, for they sense that they have nothing significant to give. If we have nothing more than textual proofs for our distinctive beliefs, we will not begin to earn a hearing, for the world wants to know what meaning and relevance our message has for their lives. As Ellen White discussed the two restored demoniacs whom Jesus sent to be the first to preach the gospel in the region of Decapolis, she noted their absence of any formal training in either content or methods. Then she added:

> But they bore in their own persons the evidence that Jesus was the Messiah. They could tell what they knew; what they themselves had seen, and heard, and felt of the power of Christ. This is what everyone can do whose heart has been touched by the grace of God. . . . As witnesses for Christ, we are to tell what we know, what we ourselves have seen and heard and felt. If we have been following Jesus step by step, we shall have something right to the point to tell concerning the way in which He has led us. We can tell how we have tested His promise, and found the promise true. We can bear witness to what we have known of the grace of Christ. This is the witness for which our Lord calls, and for want of which the world is perishing.[2]

3. *Heavy losses through apostasies will negate the influx.* Of what use is it to baptize new converts if we fail to incorporate them into responsible membership and they soon slip out "the back door"? Is not a member preserved as valuable as a convert won? If we do not promote a strong spiritual internal growth within our congregations, we will soon find that we are

working against ourselves. We may slip back faster than we progress forward. In the end we find that we have not only not grown internally, but even the numerical growth that we so eagerly sought has eluded us. We have lost everything.

What does our research show concerning indexes of spiritual growth in relationship to numerical growth rates? Is the divine counsel supported by empirical studies? Let's look at a few items:

Small Fellowship Groups

In our study of church growth in the North American Division we asked the pastors of the sample churches what percentage of their membership was meeting in small fellowship or study groups. Pastors reporting a higher percentage of their members in groups were more likely to be in churches experiencing actual growth. In fact, the relationship was the second strongest of the items on the pastoral questionnaire. We also requested the more than eight thousand members who responded to tell us their degree of involvement in small study or fellowship groups. Only about 27 percent reported heavy involvement, but they were more likely to belong to churches that were actually growing. Similar relationships showed up in the studies conducted in the Greater Atlanta area and in the Washington Conference.

Specialists like Peter Wagner tell us that one of the signs of a healthy, growing church is that it ministers not only in a large celebration-of-worship service but also in small fellowship circles, sometimes called "cells."[3] Indeed, the small group movement has represented one of the major forces in Christian churches in recent times—a major component of what has come to be called "church renewal." Our research has shown that the principle applies to Adventist churches also.

When at least a portion of the members in a congregation meet together in small groups to study the Bible, share their Christian experience, and pray for one another and the work of God in their area, a revival has begun in that church. Members find themselves motivated to use their gifts in God's service, God is able to bless the group with increase, and fewer are likely to become discouraged and forsake the church. Channels open for the Holy Spirit to work with power.

Something similar seems to have taken place in the days following Pentecost. "They devoted themselves to the apostles' teaching and to the fellowship, to the breaking of bread and to prayer. . . . They broke bread in their homes and ate together with glad and sincere hearts, praising God and enjoying the favor of all the people. And the Lord added to their number daily those who were being saved" (Acts 2:42-47). The details of this experience are rather sketchy, and we cannot demonstrate that they actually divided into small groups. Yet the kinds of things that took place and the exciting results closely reflect the small-group concept. "The formation of small companies as a basis of Christian effort has been presented to me by One who cannot err."

It makes sense! A church that displays personal warmth and caring will naturally attract people. In a huge, impersonal society, they need to feel a part of something, a member of a family. Large, formal worship services (which, however, meet their own kind of needs) cannot sustain such a sense of belonging. The division into small groups of eight to twelve members puts the personal element back in. A part of church growth? Yes. People, whether already church members or still considering membership, will gravitate toward a group that will satisfy their personal needs. This is the basic concept of the Caring Church.

Prayer Meeting

Much of the rationale for small study and fellowship groups can apply also to prayer meetings. In fact, in many churches the prayer meeting attendance may constitute the primary small group in that congregation. While it may be good for those who do attend and share, most of the membership does not receive its blessings.

We asked our pastors in North America what percentage of their membership regularly came to prayer meeting. Responses ranged from 1 percent to 98 percent (wouldn't you like to pastor *that* church?), with an average of about 25 percent. The proportion attending had a stronger correlation with kingdom growth than any other variable on the pastor survey. We also observed a relationship between prayer meeting size and actual growth. Similar findings appeared in our studies of churches in Hawaii and in the Atlanta area.

Such relationships may exist because people who have the concern to come out to a midweek prayer meeting are the kind who will work actively to convert others. It may also be that such churches have a strong spiritual life and the Lord is putting His blessing on their efforts to grow. Then too, kingdom growth means that the ratio of apostasies to baptisms is low, which is what we might expect in a spiritually motivated church.

Assurance of Being Right With God

Our survey asked members to rate the degree of their assurance that they were right with God on a continuum from "not sure" to "very certain." It is encouraging to note that among church-attending Adventists in North America, nearly two thirds rate on the certain side of the scale. Both actual and kingdom growth had a positive correlation to the feeling of certainty. Similar findings showed up in our study of church growth in the Texas Conference.

Where members feel more confident of their standing in God's sight, the church tends to grow. People cannot share what they do not have. Attempts to proclaim Adventism that are not undergirded by lives transformed and experiencing joy and satisfaction may come across as only empty words or "head" religion. When the church members know that God has forgiven, justified, and filled them with the Spirit, they will be able to tell " 'how much the Lord has done for . . . [them], and how he has had mercy on [them]' " (Mark 5:19). And listeners, now as in the days of Jesus, will respond. Ministers must make this subject crystal clear.

Standards and Devotions

Several other items, while not as strong in the research, bear mentioning. Members rated their churches as to the degree of Adventist standards observed by the group. Of course that is a highly subjective item, but it is interesting to note that it had a relationship to actual growth among the churches in Hawaii. The chapter on Dean Kelley's book will report more on this important subject.

In the NAD study 59 percent of the church-attending members reported that they usually or always have personal daily Bible study, 61 percent usually or always pray daily for the conversion of specific people, 37 percent regularly study Ellen White books, and 52 percent usually or always have daily family worship. The frequency of family worship displayed a correlation with actual growth in the Hawaiian study.

Spiritual Gifts

Perhaps the subject that best ties together internal spiritual growth with outward numerical expansion is that of spiritual gifts. " 'When he ascended on high, he . . . gave gifts to men.' . . . It was he who gave some to be apostles, some to be prophets, some to be evangelists, and some to be pastors and teachers, to prepare God's people for works of service, so that the body of Christ may be built up until we all reach unity in the faith and in the knowledge of the Son of God and become mature, attaining to the whole measure of the fullness of Christ" (Eph. 4:8-13).

The major New Testament chapters on the subject are Ephesians 4, Romans 12, and 1 Corinthians 12, which list about twenty separate gifts. Other references may raise the total by a few items. And of course, there may be other gifts that the New Testament does not specifically mention.

It seems clear that the Holy Spirit uses such gifts to bring about growth. Therefore, as the church members dedicate their lives more fully to God and allow Him to live in them through the Spirit (John 14:15-27), they will begin to receive the endowments that will make responsible church growth possible. Leaders in the church growth movement have recognized this and have given strong emphasis in recent years to the subject of spiritual gifts.[5]

In our survey of Adventist members, we asked how certain they were about what their spiritual gifts were. We found only limited correlation (black members in North America) between the question and actual or kingdom growth. This may well be, however, because only recently have Adventists begun to put importance on the subject of spiritual gifts (other than prophecy). Therefore, members have not been trained to think in terms of identifying their own particular gift(s). A new focus on this vital New Testament teaching may well signal an unprecedented surge of the church forward.

Peter Wagner has suggested five steps for discovering your spiritual gift(s):

1. Explore all the possibilities by studying the Bible and Christian literature and by talking with those who possess various gifts.

2. Experiment with as many as you can.

3. Examine your feelings to see whether you enjoy serving in that particular way.

4. Evaluate your effectiveness while you are "trying out" a gift.

5. Expect confirmation from the body of believers.[6]

Individuals within the Adventist Church have now produced new materials designed to aid in understanding and discovering spiritual gifts. Drs. Roy Naden and Robert Cruise have developed the *Spiritual Gifts Inventory* (SGI), a twelve-page self-scoring booklet, empirically developed by testing more than two thousand subjects, that can reveal in fifteen minutes the areas in which a person most probably has gifts.

Dr. Naden has followed up with *Discovering Your Spiritual Gifts,* a series of seven booklets that set out in simple-to-understand terms the New Testament teaching on the subject, with definitions, illustrations, and discussion questions for each of the Biblical gifts.

Many pastors are now using the SGI and *Discovering Your Spiritual Gifts* as the basis for a series of prayer meetings or study classes to help the membership make full use of the various gifts God has endowed the church with to fulfill its mission.[7]

In conclusion, let us say that church growth occurs as the members develop a deep, inner spiritual life. They come together to pray and praise God, meeting in small fellowship and study groups marked by loving and caring. Such

MORE THAN A NUMBERS GAME

members have assurance that God has accepted them and forgiven their sins. When they identify, accept, and use their particular spiritual gifts, God adds His blessing to their congregations with an influx of converts. Because the church has quality, He can trust it with quantity. It is a safe environment for new members.

References

[1] Ellen G. White, *Testimonies* (Mountain View, Calif.: Pacific Press Pub. Assn., 1948), vol. 6, p. 371.
[2] ———, *The Desire of Ages* (Mountain View, Calif.: Pacific Press Pub. Assn., 1940), p. 340.
[3] C. Peter Wagner, *Your Church Can Grow*, pp. 97-109.
[4] Ellen G. White, *Testimonies*, vol. 7, pp. 21, 22.
[5] For example, see C. Peter Wagner, *Your Spiritual Gifts Can Help Your Church Grow* (Glendale, Calif.: Regal Books, 1979).
[6] *Ibid.*, pp. 116-133.
[7] For price lists and ordering information, write: Institute of Church Ministry, Andrews University, Berrien Springs, Michigan 49103.

4

A Message From Kelley

One of the major religious phenomena of our times took place in the last half of the 1960s and throughout the 1970s. After many years of membership increase, most of the large denominations in the United States stopped growing and began to shrink. Church leaders and sociologists of religion have been seeking answers to this puzzling situation, and the results of their search have filled a considerable portion of the religious literature of our day. Most have held that church growth and decline are largely the result of contextual factors (those outside of the church and its control) such as value shifts in the population, neighborhood changes, and local economic trends. And we can marshal some persuasive evidence in favor of the strong influence of contextual factors.

But in 1972, a bombshell exploded on the scene with the publication of the book *Why Conservative Churches Are Growing: A Study in Sociology of Religion*.[1] The book quickly became one of the most widely read and controversial religious publications of the decade (a second edition appeared in 1977). The author was Dean Kelley, a Methodist minister and an executive with the National Council of Churches.

Kelley largely ignored contextual explanations and focused on institutional factors (those reasons that are internal to the church and are aspects of its life and functioning over which it has some control). He pointed out that during the same period when at least ten mainline denominations in America had lost members each year, other churches like the Southern Baptist Convention, the Church of the Nazarene, the Salvation Army, the Mormons, the Jehovah's Witnesses, and the Seventh-day Adventists had grown rapidly.[2]

Kelley proposed:

> What religion needs is someone to do for it what Freud did for sex: to show that it has its own elemental drives, dynamics, and necessities that are .not to be explained in terms of "extraneous" factors such as economics, geography, demographics, or climate. Though environmental influences may sway the more attenuated forms of religious life, they have much less effect upon the "purer" or more vigorous forms—which some people have been accustomed to look down upon as "fanatical" sects.[3]

The Business of Religion

Ecumenical churches do not lose members because they engage in social-action programs, Kelley insists, but because they neglect the one business that gives the church a unique role among social institutions: *explaining the meaning of life in ultimate terms.*[4] Other groups may have programs similar to those of the church, but only religion dispenses meaning.

But we must not confuse meanings with ideas, vague concepts, or notions. Addressed to persons, meanings demand something of them. In a brilliant chapter Kelley argues that unless a principle is worth staking the life upon and paying the price for, it does not have much meaning.[5] When meanings are "used for detached, abstract speculation, they cease to be meanings and become mere notions: ideas that have lost the power to change lives, to recruit movements, to explain things convincingly."[6] Therefore, "the quality that enables religious meanings to take hold is not their rationality, their logic, their surface credibility, but rather the *demand* they make upon their adherents and the degree to which that demand is met by *commitment.*"[7]

In the preface to his second edition, Kelley looks back on the five years of controversy that swirled around his book and muses that his main theme (the business of religion is to explain the ultimate meaning of life) has encountered little opposition, but that reaction to the corollary theme has been less congenial. We may state his second theme as "the quality which makes one system of ultimate meaning more convincing than another is not its content but its seriousness/ strictness/ costliness/ bindingness."[8]

Traits of Strictness

Kelley gives a rather detailed description of those evidences of social strength and traits of strictness that characterize a strong religion.[9] We may sum them up as (1) commitment to the group's goals, (2) discipline—willingness to obey, (3) missionary zeal, (4) absolutism—belief that "we have the truth and all others are in error," (5) conformity— intolerance of deviance or dissent, and (6) fanaticism—far more likely to preach its message to the world than to listen to what others have to say.

Similarly, he describes the evidences of social weakness and traits of leniency that seem to form part of a weak religion.[10] They are: (1) lukewarmness—indecisiveness, (2) individualism, (3) reserve—reluctance to expose one's personal beliefs or to impose them on others, (4) relativism—no group has a monopoly on truth, (5) diversity—appreciation of individual differences, and (6) dialogue—willingness to listen to points of view held by others.

Kelley thus arrives at what he considers to be the minimal maxims of seriousness or strictness:

Those who are serious about their faith:

1. Do not confuse it with other beliefs/loyalties/practices, or mingle them together indiscriminately, or pretend they are alike, of equal merit, or mutually compatible if they are not.

2. Make high demands of those admitted to the organization that bears the faith, and do not include or allow to continue within it those who are not fully committed to it.

3. Do not consent to, encourage, or indulge any violations

of its standards of belief or behavior by its professed adherents.

4. Do not keep silent about it, apologize for it, or let it be treated as though it made no difference, or should make no difference, in their behavior or in their relationships with others.[11]

Thus Kelley does not attempt to deal with the rightness or the wrongness of a particular religious content. His thesis concerns itself only with what the church does with the content it professes to believe in.

Based on his descriptions of strictness versus leniency, Kelley has rated twenty-seven American churches on an exclusivist-ecumenical gradient ranging from Black Muslims and Jehovah's Witnesses to Unitarian-Universalists. He placed Seventh-day Adventists seventh from the exclusivist extreme, just below the Mormons but above all mainline churches.[12]

THE EXCLUSIVIST-ECUMENICAL GRADIENT

Black Muslims
Jehovah's Witnesses
Evangelicals and Pentecostals
Orthodox Jews
Churches of Christ
Latter-day Saints (Mormons)
Seventh-day Adventists
Church of God
Church of Christ, Scientist
Southern Baptist Convention
Lutheran Church-Missouri Synod
American Lutheran Church
Roman Catholic Church
Conservative Jews
Russian Orthodox
Greek Orthodox
Lutheran Church in America
Southern Presbyterian Church
Reformed Church in America
Episcopal Church

A MESSAGE FROM KELLEY

American Baptist Convention
United Presbyterian Church
United Methodist Church
United Church of Christ
Reform Jews
Ethical Culture Society
Unitarian-Universalists

You will readily see that Kelley is not talking so much about *conservative* churches as a description of their theology as he is about *strict* churches as a measure of their commitment to their faith and adherence to a distinctive life style (although strict churches usually do happen to be also conservative in theology). His original title for the book was "Why Strict Churches Are Strong," but the publisher insisted on the more marketable title.

Yet somehow the idea of a strict church does not seem in harmony with the tenor of the times. Kelley himself, whose vocation lies in the field of religious liberty, admits to being uncomfortable with some of the concepts he proclaims. This is especially true when one thinks of the excesses and persecutions often associated with strict religions. But, he continues, it is not necessary that a strict church be harsh or unloving or that it violate religious liberty. It must simply be firm in protecting the essential things that it stands for. By way of illustration he states:

> If a voluntary association is formed to abolish capital punishment, it does not knowingly include among its members those who *favor* capital punishment. They are free to form their own association, which in its turn will exclude advocates of abolition. Both groups will be especially careful to limit the inner circles of leadership to those who wholly support the organization's objectives. [13]

Religious organizations often lower their standards for admitting and retaining members in hopes of having a broader appeal to more people. But the message from Kelley is that they thereby *lose* their attractiveness. The most liberal, nondemanding denominations have suffered the greatest decline in recent years. Therefore, churches must use the only means they have to preserve their purpose and character—

45

the power of the gate, the power to control who may enter and remain and on what conditions. Kelley proposes that we may learn how to use this power from the practices of the early Anabaptists and Wesleyans:

1. In no haste to take anyone into membership, they required a lengthy period of preparation.

2. The tests of membership were attitudinal and behavioral rather than solely or chiefly doctrinal.

3. Membership was conditional upon continuing faithfulness.

4. Members made their life pilgrimage together in small groups, aiding and encouraging one another.

5. No one who had not undertaken the rigorous training and accepted the obedience and discipline of the group had any voice in making its decisions. [14]

A most solemn message! But would it prove true under the rigors of empirical research?

Testing Kelley's Theories

Dean Hoge, sociologist at Catholic University and a specialist in church growth from a sociological perspective, designed a study to test Kelley's propositions.[15] Twenty-one experts rated sixteen of the largest churches in the United States on eight dimensions. The group included church historians, sociologists of religion, denominational and ecumenical leaders, and seminary educators. All were eminent in their respective fields.

The ratings were on scales of one to seven whose poles were defined; the time period covered was 1966 to 1975. The eight dimensions consisted of the following:

1. Strength of Ethnic Identity
2. Theological Conservatism or Liberalism
3. Attitudes Toward Ecumenism
4. Centralized or Congregational Polity
5. Emphasis on Local and Community Evangelism
6. Involvement in Social Action
7. Emphasis on Distinctive Life Style and Morality
8. Attitude Toward Pluralism of Beliefs Among Members[16]

The study averaged the ratings of the experts to give each church a mean rating on each of the eight dimensions. The Seventh-day Adventist Church was one of the sixteen denominations examined. It is interesting to note how it did in comparison with other churches (none of the experts was an Adventist).

Adventists received the rank of second most conservative theologically (after the Assemblies of God) and the third most negative toward ecumenism (after the Mormons and Churches of Christ). It stood the fourth highest on emphasis on evangelism (Southern Baptists, Assemblies of God, and Mormons led) and fifth from the bottom in involvement in social action. The group rated Adventists the second highest in distinctive life style (after Mormons). On attitudes toward pluralism the SDA Church was number one in demanding strict standards from its members.[17]

Some of our readers may feel that the study has judged us too harshly or too easily on certain items, but that is the way they perceived us. Frankly, we wonder whether the experts did not have Adventists of bygone generations in mind, and whether the modern church really deserves such high ratings on items like distinctive life style and attitude toward pluralism.

Hoge next compiled growth rates on the sixteen churches for the decade 1965-1975. With a 36 percent growth, the Adventist Church ranked second, just behind the Assemblies of God (37 percent).[18] The study then correlated the mean ratings on the eight dimensions with the decadal growth rates. While it obtained low relationships for congregational polity and ethnic identity, it found the following extremely high correlations for the other six variables: Theological Liberalism (-.86), Ecumenism (-.87), Emphasis on Evangelism (.93), Involvement in Social Action (-.88), Distinctive Life Style (.97), and Affirms Pluralism (-.84). In the case of negative correlations the trait shows an inverse relationship with growth. For example, high ecumenism accompanies low growth rates.[19]

The study led Hoge to conclude that

> the denominational characteristics attributed by Kelley to growing denominations are strongly upheld by independent ratings of experts. The factors Kelley stressed most . . . came out the strongest. . . . These six represent slight variations on a single axis, which might be called "liberal-pluralistic-culture-affirming" on one end, "conservative-disciplined-distinctive from culture" on the other end. Denominations near the latter end grow more than others and tend to have higher levels of church attendance than others. They also have higher rates of per capita contributions. We conclude that denominational growth is indeed closely associated with certain denominational traits during the 1965-1975 period.[20]

A Warning for Seventh-day Adventists

Since Adventists seem to be doing quite well compared to the mainline churches, we might assume a certain smugness. But wait! They once stood where we do now. Kelley goes on to explain that his model is not static but dynamic. "A strong organization which loses its strictness will also lose its strength." And the relationship is degenerative as well as dynamic. "Strictness tends to deteriorate into leniency, which results in social weakness in place of strength."[21] He quotes John Wesley's Law:

> *Wherever riches have increased, the essence of religion has decreased in the same proportion.* Therefore, I do not see how it is possible, in the nature of things, for any revival of religion to continue long. For religion must necessarily produce both industry and frugality, and these cannot but produce riches. But as riches increase, so will pride, anger, and love of the world in all its branches. . . . *Is there no way to prevent this—this continual decay of pure religion?*[22]

The quotation identifies the danger of the second-generation syndrome. In the early stages of a movement, Kelley explains, "nonconformity is often punished by peers rather than by leaders. All the members feel a personal and direct responsibility for preserving the purity or discipline or purpose of the organization, . . . often in a loving yet firm way; members will even confess and correct their own errors for the sake of the movement and their own wholehearted participation in it."[23] He calls this quality "stringency." But later in the history of the organization members lose this motivation and let the responsibility fall on the professionals. "Discipline is imposed by the stern leader upon shamed and sheepish members." [24] Kelley terms the behavior "stricture."

Has the Adventist Church been slowly slipping from strictness to leniency, from seriousness to lukewarmness, from stringency to stricture, from culture-denying to culture-affirming, from strength to weakness? We would not presume to sit in judgment, nor is this a plea for "witch hunts" and harsh un-Christlike methods. It is rather a call for self-examination. An editorial in the *Adventist Review* quotes Dr. Jon Johnston, of Pepperdine University, as saying:

> "Sociological studies show that when persons are convinced that their society is rejecting them because of their religious values, they tend to cling to those values even more tenaciously. Why? Because they perceive that their faith is costing them dearly. What is worth sacrificing for is worth cherishing. . . . On the other hand, sociologists tell us that when individuals sense that their culture no longer repudiates their values and, instead, elevates their status for following such principles, the following things are likely to increasingly occur: Society's values are embraced, while religious standards are relaxed. . . . Retaining and even accelerating societal approval of itself becomes a primary goal of the religious body." [25]

Certainly popularity may prove to be a danger to a church in terms of its social strength and, paradoxically, in its probability of growth.

Another measure of seriousness is support of missions. In 1970, Adventists in North America gave an amount equal to 12.7 percent of their tithe to foreign missions. By 1980, the figure had dropped to 9.6 percent.[26] Does the steady decline over a period of years in per capita giving to missions say anything about our commitment to our faith?

It would be a mistake for church leadership to prescribe an exact list of the beliefs and behaviors that pastors and members must conform to. Yet disaster awaits the opposite extreme, for history certainly does reveal something of the dangers of pluralism within a religious movement. When the umbrella has become big enough to cover most people and their divergent beliefs and behaviors, the resulting content and life style has had much of its unique meaning stripped away from it.

All of this has a great deal to do with church growth, for, as Kelley reminds us, unless a religious movement dispenses ultimate meanings that one cannot obtain elsewhere, and unless its followers consider such meanings so valuable that they willingly commit their all to them, it is not likely that many will be attracted to it. They will come only for what they cannot secure more easily somewhere else.

References

[1] Dean M. Kelley, *Why Conservative Churches Are Growing: A Study in Sociology of Religion*, second edition (San Francisco: Harper and Row, 1977).

[2] *Ibid.*, pp. 24, 25.

[3] *Ibid.*, p. viii.

[4] *Ibid.*, p. 37.

[5] *Ibid.*, pp. 47-55.

[6] *Ibid.*, p. 52.

[7] *Ibid.*, p. 53.

[8] *Ibid.*, p. xii.

[9] *Ibid.*, pp. 58-81.

[10] *Ibid.*, pp. 82-85.

[11] *Ibid.*, p. 121.

[12] *Ibid.*, p. 89.

[13] *Ibid.*, p. 123.

[14] *Ibid.*, pp. 125-127.

[15] Dean R. Hoge, "A Test of Theories of Denominational Growth and Decline," in *Understanding Church Growth and Decline: 1950-1978*, pp. 179-197.

[16] *Ibid.*, pp. 183, 184.

[17] *Ibid.*, p. 185.

[18] *Ibid.*, p. 187.

[19] *Ibid.*, p. 191.

[20] *Ibid.*, pp. 192, 193.

[21] Kelley, *op. cit.*, p. 96.

[22] *Ibid.*, p. 55.

[23] *Ibid.*, p. 109.

[24] *Ibid.*, pp. 109, 110.

[25] Leo R. Van Dolson, "Popularity a Mixed Blessing," *Adventist Review*, Oct. 15, 1981, pp. 13, 14.

[26] Bruce Bauer, "Needed: A Renewed Commitment to Missions," *Adventist Review*, Sept. 10, 1981, pp. 7, 8.

5

The Adventist Church:
Three Distinctive Experiences

The Seventh-day Adventist Church has historically identified itself with Christ's commission to communicate the gospel effectively, a task church leaders have found increasingly complex as their ministry has expanded to a growing number of ethnic groups in North America and throughout the world. To perceive itself accurately, the church must recognize and respond to differences among various ethnic groups within Seventh-day Adventism. Developments in the past decade have made clear that Adventism in North America consists of at least three distinct churches: white, Hispanic, and black.[1]

The chart on page 52 illustrates the major differences among the three groups within North American Adventism. The information comes from our church growth survey of the North American Division.[2]

Such data helps to emphasize the distinctive identity of each of the three ethnic churches. In brief, it reveals that the Hispanic church in North America is the youngest and fastest growing, with fewer second-generation Adventist members. The black church, growing slower than the Hispanic, has a

	White	Hispanic	Black
Total surveyed	5,275	997	2,063
Average church growth			
Kingdom	3.6%	11.7%	5.6%
Actual	5.6%	14.8%	6.8%
Age groups			
35 and below	34%	50%	48%
50 and above	39%	20%	24%
Percent having SDA parent(s)	52%	31%	39%
Number of years baptized SDA			
5 or less	20%	48%	34%
11 or more	65%	30%	44%

slightly older profile and a somewhat higher percentage of second-generation members. The white church is the slowest growing—it is considerably older, having almost 30 percent more members 50 years of age and over than the Hispanic church, with an equally greater percentage of second-generation members.

Treating the church as a whole obscures these important variations in growth rate, age, years baptized, and percent of second-generation members. Highlighting them allows leaders to comprehend the issues faced by each group and enables them to develop specific strategies tailored to them. It would be naive and counterproductive to develop policy or programs that do not take into consideration the differences among North American ethnic groups.

White Church

Without doubt, the white church in North America faces a problem of old age. During the decade of the 1980s, it must focus on attracting and activating youth and young adults. This will require more than token statements about the belief that the youth will finish the church's mission. To make this possible, the church will need to allow youth to undergo the struggle of expressing themselves in the terms of their own generation. It is impossible for a new generation to communicate effectively something they have not experienced and understood in their own terms. We do not mean that the church should radically alter its doctrines, but that those doctrines need personalizing for the present generation. Older Adventists can ill afford to restrict or overreact to this process; they must facilitate and participate in the redefining. The translation of Scripture can illustrate what we mean. As time alters words and thought patterns, an older translation of Scripture is often less effective in communicating truth to a new age. Thus, when a new translation appears, the new generation embraces it. Truth is not lost or abandoned, but put in contemporary terms, and, in many cases, the new translations are more accurate than the old, because of archeological advances.

But any redefining is a traumatic experience for the older generation. It resembles that faced by parents and their adolescents. Parents sometimes find themselves gripped with fear that the adolescent will reject all that the family holds dear. If they allow this fear to control them, parents may delay the struggle for adult faith and enhance the possibility that their child will actually throw over their faith or continue in an immature conforming one. We must view the questions of adolescents as attempts to define a personal faith identity and meet them with open discussion, from which both the adolescent and parent will probably benefit. Mutual respect and an adult faith identity will result.

Many of the present theological discussions in the white church take on a much more hopeful note when viewed from such a perspective. While it is true that some of the discussions give cause for concern, a far greater number provide reason for hope—the hope of a generation struggling to define its adult faith. The question for the older Adventist is "How will we relate to this process?" The pivotal question for those engaged in redefinition must always be "Will our energies become absorbed in theological discussion to the neglect of Christian mission?" The greatest tragedy would be for both old and young to engage in internal theological warfare within the confines of institutional cloisters—dialoguing only with one another—while the world goes on outside, oblivious to us! It is well for us to remember that the authors of the New Testament wrote and explained its theology in the midst of witness. To assert that we must get our theology together before we engage in witness is, in itself, another form of perfectionism. Christianity is a heart relationship with Jesus Christ—the relationship can be perfect, but the words with which we express it cannot.

The greatest strength of the white church arises from the financial commitment of its members to evangelism. When asked how often they provide financial support for local evangelism, 49 percent of the white members said "Always," compared to 43 percent of the hispanic members and 37 percent of the black members. Understanding the reasons for such a strong stewardship pattern will assist leaders of black and hispanic congregations in solving some of the economic pressures of rapid church growth. We should note here that such reasons may have no necessary relationship to income.

Hispanic Church

The most prominent feature of the Hispanic church in our study was its relative youth. The issues such a young, rapidly growing church must face include assimilating new members, meeting the facility needs of an increasing number of worshipers, and providing pastoral care and responding to problems created by second-generation cultural melting. Some evidence indicates that the Hispanic church has already begun differentiating into Spanish-speaking and English-speaking worship preferences.

The second-generation melting problems tend to occur when children of Spanish-speaking parents become integrated into the English-speaking culture. Cultural melting occurs more rapidly among Christians, for, as Wesley pointed out, when people accept Christ, they become more honest, more faithful. Therefore, they work harder, save more money, and waste less, with the net result that they climb the socioeconomic ladder. Church growth specialist Donald McGavran has labeled the process "redemption and lift."

Redemption and lift can halt church growth if the second generation moves out of its old community and desires to become integrated into English-speaking society. Second-generation members may want their children to enjoy some of

the benefits of English-speaking societies in order to ensure
that they will receive better jobs and enjoy a higher standard
of living. Adjusting to this sociological trend will require the
prayerful and thoughtful leadership of hispanic pastors.

The overall strengths of the Hispanic church are its
relative youth, member involvement in giving Bible studies,
church unity, and member involvement in small study
groups. The following chart illustrates these characteristics as
compared to black and white congregations.

	White	*Hispanic*	*Black*
Percent involved in a witness program	52%	50%	63%
Percent involved in community services	33%	39%	41%
Percent who held Bible studies with a non-SDA this year	23%	52%	41%
Percent rating the church as united versus divided	60%	72%	51%
Percent who are regularly meeting in small study groups	11%	19%	13%
How many people have you been responsible for bringing into the church in the past three years?			
Unaware of any	64%	38%	49%
1 person	12%	16%	16%
2-5 persons	12%	26%	19%
6-10 persons	1%	4%	2%
10 or more persons	1%	10%	3%

Black Church

The black church in North America is neither as young as
the Hispanic nor as old as the white. It tends to share more of
the characteristics of the Hispanic church. A key insight in
reviewing the black church profile comes from noting the
upward mobility of the young adults of age 25 to 30. This
group is exploding into the middle-income bracket, and
leadership must carefully study its impact on the future of the
church. While the Hispanic church may find "redemption

and lift" an issue of future church growth, the black church is already experiencing it to a large degree. If present trends continue, young adult blacks may move from their original neighborhoods to establish residence in middle-class urban areas. Should that occur, the decade of the 1980s could see an increase of commuter church members and a decrease in the number who form an integral part of the neighborhood in which the church building is located.

Lack of effectiveness in ministering to the neighborhood is a symptom of church growth halting as a result of redemption and lift. If the church attempts to "cure" the symptoms by increasing the programs rather than by establishing a personal presence and relationship with the community, the prevailing attitude becomes one of "us and them" between the community and the church. People from the community feel less inclined to come to the church, and a slowing or suspension of growth takes place.

Some may argue that the black cultural experience has a strong enough identity with one's original neighborhood to resist the trend. But it appears certain that the mobility of young black professionals will tend to break down home-community ties as options in the job market demand relocation.

An increased affluence opens the door to middle-class urban communities. One can test this trend by asking, "Are the young adults in our church living within walking distance of the church?" and "Where does the pastor live in relation to it?"

The greatest impact of upward mobility in the black congregation could be in the area of ministering to youth. The increasing affluence of the young black challenges the role of the church in his life. Where once the church was its center, increased income allows him to fill his life with entertainment and secular activity. Frequently the church has countered this by seeking to appeal to the social side of youth, competing with the world by offering a church version of entertainment. Athletic events, recreation, movies, and socials come to characterize such a program, supplanting the strong evangelistic emphasis of the past with a "fun and games" search for relevance. Black youth leaders should realize that this trend in the white church has resulted in the collapse of the senior youth program formerly known as the MV Society. Black youth leaders should lay strategies to retain the evangelistic and fellowship nature of their youth groups and the church at large.

The chief strength of the black church is the large degree of involvement of its members in community service and all types of witness activities. The chart on page 55 compares the involvement of witnessing among the white, Hispanic, and black groups.

Such active participation in witnessing is a prime reason for the current evangelistic vitality of the black church.

In summary, the Adventist Church in North America consists of at least three distinct experiences. If we treat these differing churches as a homogenous unit without regard to their individual strengths and weaknesses, they will suffer a common malaise that will continue to baffle administrators and impede real growth. But on the other hand, if leadership recognizes the strengths and weaknesses of the white, black, and Hispanic churches, it will be able to design services and resources and enact policies for each in keeping with demonstrable need. Such a "customized" approach to policy-making does not imply a competitive or superior attitude on the part of any group—rather a beneficial shaping of the ingredients that have made each church strong.

References

[1] The emergence of a strong Asian Adventist population in North America calls for church growth research among this group. To date, major research among Adventist Asians has not been undertaken.

[2] Roger Dudley and Des Cummings, "Church Growth in the North American Division."

6

Owning Goals

Once upon a time a certain conference determined to take seriously its responsibility to reach the multitudes within its area with the good news of the gospel and to incorporate as many as possible of them within the body of Christ's church. The coordinator of evangelism and the officers worked together to formulate a plan. The conference committee adopted it. Then the leadership informed the pastors in the field of it by letter.

The letter stated that the conference had set a goal to baptize eight hundred people during the next calendar year, and it explained how they could easily reach it. The conference asked each district to set aside four special baptism days—one in each quarter. The last Sabbath in March they would designate "Youth Baptism Day," and the emphasis would be on young people joining the church. In June each congregation would hold "Homecoming Day," when the members would welcome ex-Adventists back to the fold. Then in September the churches would celebrate "Families United Day," a time when the relatives of church members could become a part of God's family. Finally, December would witness "Personal Interest Day," when the lay members would rejoice in the harvest from their Bible studies and personal witnessing during the past year.

The letter went on to lay out a mathematical formula for achieving the baptismal goal. The conference consisted of thirty-six districts. If each district would baptize three people on each of the special days, it would equal twelve over the year's time. Multiply twelve by the thirty-six districts, and the conference would have added 432 new members. Next, the conference employed three full-time evangelists. Each had pledged to bring in one hundred new members through the various campaigns they would hold during the target year, bringing the total baptisms up to 732. Of course, the baptisms by the evangelists could not duplicate those brought in on the special days, even though some of the local congregations would hold public evangelistic services during these "special" times. Finally, the letter pointed out that the conference contained eighty-seven churches, and if each congregation would baptize one new convert during the whole year in addition to the twelve per district and those of the evangelists, the total number of baptisms from all three sources would total 819, thus topping the eight hundred goal for the year.

Is It Proper to Set Goals?

Frankly, for reasons we will soon discuss, some of the pastors felt uneasy over the plan. But we would like to begin by commending the conference leadership for taking its mission seriously. It has been said that it is better to aim at a high goal and miss it than to aim at nothing and hit it. Experience almost universally reveals that we cannot accomplish anything worthwhile if we simply take what comes. If we do not plan for success and focus our efforts upon specific targets, we will have little to show for our busyness.

Our study of church growth in the North American Division asked pastors to state their churches' growth goals for the year in terms of a percentage of their present membership. Responses ranged from twenty-five churches that had set no goal at all to one church that had set its growth goal at 100 percent of its membership. The higher goals had a significant correlation with the actual growth rate and with the number of baptisms. The picture became even more striking when we isolated the white churches from the total sample. The relationship between the setting of high growth goals and the rate of actual growth was one of the strongest we found in the study.[1]

Other, more localized, studies further confirm our findings. In studying the Adventist churches in Hawaii, we discovered that a higher baptismal goal increases the likelihood of a real rise in the number of local members. Growing churches averaged a baptismal goal seven percentage points higher than their nongrowing sister ones. It suggests that congregations tend to reach higher when they aim higher.[2]

In the Atlanta, Georgia, area, church baptismal and church growth goals were among the most significant factors that distinguished high-growth from low-growth congregations. High-growth churches averaged a baptismal goal of 33 percent of their membership, contrasting sharply with the average of 13 percent set by low-growth churches. The difference was even greater with church growth goals. There the figures were 73 percent and 7 percent, respectively. A similar picture emerges when we compare the churches on the basis of kingdom growth.[3]

Thus we should not criticize the setting of goals for baptisms or for church growth. Such goals are not only permissible; they are necessary for the church to accomplish its mission. Congregations that want to grow and are willing to sacrifice to attain growth will likely have clear goals. Having a high numerical objective for expansion increases the probability of real growth. The question we must consider here is not whether churches should have goals, but How should we set them?

The Problem With Goals From on High

When we examine the plan of our well-meaning conference officials, we discover at least three defects that may mar its effectiveness:

The flow of people into the church. The Lord does not bring people into the church in neat little categories, each assigned to a particular quarter of the year. The working of the Holy Spirit is likely to be far more diverse than that. Still, it is the plan's least serious fault, and it may be well to have certain special days of emphasis, though they should not constitute so major a portion of the church's growth strategy.

The fairness of the goal distribution. Here is a more serious criticism. Let us suppose that the conference has a large institutional church of one thousand members. It has a senior pastor, two associates, and a membership with a good mix of business and professional people. The pastor studies the letter from the conference office and calculates his share of the eight hundred baptisms. "Let's see, now. Three for each quarter makes twelve, plus one for my one church. Hmm—I guess my share is thirteen baptisms. Well, I think that's reasonable enough. My youth pastor has twelve of our church school students in his baptismal class right now. We won't have *any* trouble making that. No sweat!"

But that same conference also has a young pastor with three churches scattered over a sparsely populated area sometimes known as the "boonies." His "large" church has fifty members, the mid-sized one has twenty-two members, plus he has charge of a company of seven members. Most of the people are elderly—a majority of them retired. None of the congregations has any well-educated or professional people; there are only a few young children, and no teen-agers.

This pastor also calculates his share of the conference goal. "Twelve for the district plus one for each of my three churches—fifteen! Where am I ever going to find fifteen people to baptize around here? I'm in big trouble."

We're sure that you'll agree that any plan that calls for a pastor with a total membership of seventy-nine members and no help to baptize *more* people in a year—or even as many—than a pastor with one thousand members and an adequate staff has a basic inequity. Surely you wouldn't suggest the same goals for churches in sparsely populated or decaying communities as those in growing, vibrant ones. Of course, the conference planners did not set out to be unfair.

But that is the inevitable result of any system that attempts to formulate the goals at the top and pass them down to the component parts. It is simply impossible to adjust for all the variables that make the situation of any particular congregation different from that of its fellow churches.

The place where goals should be set. The third defect in the conference plan is the most serious of all. It ignores the fundamental principle that the people who will be expected to reach them must establish the goals. It is not merely a nice show of consideration for the feelings of another, but a law of human behavior, involving what we like to call goal ownership. If people do not have a share in the making of goals and plans to reach them, they will not feel committed to them—they will not "own" those goals.

Consider what usually happens. The pastor takes the letter from the conference and dutifully announces the plan and the goal to the congregation. We will grant that his enthusiasm and salesmanship will play some part in the reaction (but remember, he doesn't "own" the goal either). The typical member in the typical congregation nods his head and thinks, This is something the conference wants, or, This is something the pastor thinks is important. He probably doesn't get too excited about it.

Goal-ownership theory holds that when goals are set "up there" someplace, the people "up there" own them. The members may or may not cooperate with the plans, depending upon their overall commitment to the church, but they will not likely take them too seriously. After all, they really didn't have anything to do with them.

How to Turn the Situation Around

Conference leadership should encourage each congregation to study its local situation, decide what God would have that church to do to fulfill of its mission, set growth goals, and lay wise plans for attaining them. Does that mean that the pastor establishes the objectives? Does he go to the January workers' meeting and, after listening to a stirring appeal from the conference president, jot down on a slip of paper the number of people whom he hopes to baptize during the coming year? Well, that does put goal ownership one step closer to the place where the work must be done, but unless the pastor intends to do it all by himself, he had better get his members to "own" those goals with him.

Another thing. Too often that figure the pastor wrote on the slip of paper at the meeting came right off the top of his head. He did not arrive at it through a serious study of the needs of the community or the resources of the church. The pastor had no well-formulated strategies for obtaining the baptisms. Goals not undergirded by reality and backed up with concrete plans are worse than useless. They lead us only to fool ourselves into thinking we are going to do something when, in fact, we are not.

Ideally, the process begins with the individual member setting a personal soul-winning goal for the year. Our research showed that kingdom growth correlated with the number of members setting personal evangelism targets among Hawaiian churches[4] and that as more members set personal goals, apostasies decreased in Spanish churches in the North American Division.[5]

In the next chapter we will describe in some detail how a Caring Church goes about setting goals and laying plans to reach them. Let us say here that the process should involve various committees, the church board, and the full membership as far as possible. The process includes (1) a study of the community and its needs, (2) an assessment of the congregation's resources, (3) the hammering out of goals and strategies with input from every member possible, and (4) a vote on the plans by the full church. Such a process maximizes the possibility of goal ownership.

At this point the congregation presents its plans for the year (including the growth goal) to the conference. When the conference receives all the church goals, it compiles them into the conference target. The various conference goals make up the union conference goal, and so on up the line to the division and finally to the General Conference itself. Goals that move up from the grass roots may lead to a higher combined total than those sent down from the top, and they will much more likely reach fulfillment because the people who will have to do the work now "own" them.

Does the conference have any part to play, therefore, or any responsibility in the process of goal setting? Of course. But the conference cannot be most effective in setting the objectives—or even in suggesting them. Rather, the conference functions would seem to best fall along the following lines:

1. The conference inspires congregations to engage in the goal-setting process and gently prods them into action.

2. The conference staff trains congregations in the procedure of goal-setting through in-service education for the pastor and through meeting with the church board and other committees as necessary.

3. The conference provides a bank of resources in the form of materials, methods, and programs that local congregations can utilize.

4. The conference helps churches to check out the appropriateness of the goals they have chosen. For example, if the pastor of a large church, rich in resources, reports that his congregation has set a goal to baptize five people in the coming year, the president or Ministerial director may well sit down with the minister and review how the church arrived at its goal. Thus the conference aids the local church in a process of reality testing concerning its goals. But this would not take place only when the target was obviously too low. The president might well show the pastor how the goal was unrealistically high, given the resources and the strategies designed to meet it.

5. The conference serves as a source of accountability to encourage congregations to keep pressing toward the goals that *they* have chosen.

The Tyranny of Goals

Some people are afraid of goals, and indeed, when they become more important than human considerations, they can turn into tyrants. Certainly we must evaluate our congregations on other considerations than mere numbers. Yet it is not wrong to set a reasonable goal as a target for which to shoot if the process is based on sound research and the people who must do the work have been included and are committed to it. Setting a goal is a prerequisite to being able to measure what one has actually accomplished.

The danger to avoid is letting the goal become an end in itself, so that we feel that we have to baptize that many, come what may. Focusing on numbers to the exclusion of making responsible disciples can lead to unfaithfulness to our calling. Some, in an attempt to reach a goal (usually set for them by someone else), have baptized people they knew were not ready, or they used high-pressure sales techniques. It is important to remember that goals are not an end in themselves, but only a means to an end—bringing glory to God and helping to finish His mission on earth.

Lay members must sense that the church belongs to them and that they are responsible for accomplishing its mission. When they get involved in the process of goal setting from start to finish, they will "own" the goals and will freely give of their time, talents, and treasure to reach them. The church will come alive, and its task will soon be finished.

References

[1] Roger Dudley and Des Cummings, "Church Growth in the North American Division," pp. 62, 64, 76, 91, 129, 130.

[2] Greg Clark, Roger Dudley, and Des Cummings, "Church Growth in the Hawaiian Mission," pp. 16-18.

[3] ——, "Church Growth in Greater Atlanta," pp. 17-20, 25, 26, 28, 29.

[4] ——, "Church Growth in the Hawaiian Mission," p. 56.

[5] Dudley and Cummings, *op. cit.*, p. 116.

7

A Model for Church Planning

In the previous chapter we argued that church baptismal and growth goals should originate at the local congregation level and involve input from as large a proportion of the membership as possible. But how is this to be done? What methods will allow it to be a smooth and effective process, resulting in the members themselves "owning" the goals and, under the blessing of the Holy Spirit, reaching them? We would like to propose a model that we have arrived at by combining material from several sources.

The Fundamental Elements

As a result of the various church growth studies it has conducted, the Institute of Church Ministry has designed a survey instrument for the Adventist pastor. Three of the questions have particular relevance to this chapter. They ask the pastor whether or not his church has (1) specific written objectives, (2) planned methods to reach them, and (3) a functioning evangelism council.

In a series of research studies we have found that one or more of these items has correlated significantly with various indexes of church growth. For example, in a study of all the churches in the Washington Conference, we found all three items related to actual growth, written objectives to kingdom growth, planned methods to a decrease in the number of apostasies, and an evangelism council to an increase in baptisms.[1]

Similarly, in the North American Division written objectives showed a significant correlation with actual growth among the white churches, and with kingdom growth in Spanish churches and in the total sample. The presence of an evangelism council had a relationship with kingdom growth in the total sample and with a decrease in the number of apostasies in white churches.[2] We observed similar correlations among the churches of the Hawaiian Conference.[3]

The research has led us to conclude that churches that have specific written objectives in the various areas of congregational life, planned methods to reach them, and a functioning evangelism council to plan a coordinated evangelistic program will probably baptize more converts than average for their size and will more likely experience rapid actual and kingdom growth. These three items are the fundamentals that a church uses to set its goals and plan its strategies.

A Plan for Planning

The North American Division has described its philosophy of church organization for mission in the booklet *Dynamics of Church Growth*.[4] The four basic steps to Faith Action Advance are Planning, Equipping, Implementing, and Evaluating (see page 5). Planning the mission must take priority. Moving ahead without wise plans will be counterproductive. This chapter will deal with the planning phase of the church's work.

We will now give the various steps in goal setting that our model incorporates. First, though, we must note that the pastor should not decide on the goal-setting steps by himself—even though the purpose is to involve the membership. Here is the place for the pastor to work with the evangelism council or church board. He asks the council to recommend the steps that the church will take to arrive at the goals and the plans to implement them. The pastor may present the model given here for discussion, but he should offer it tentatively. The council must have full opportunity for revisions, additions, and deletions so that the procedures represent its will. From there, the procedures should go to the church board for ratification (unless the board has been functioning as the evangelism council).

Motivation

Once the church has adopted procedures, the first step in the model will probably involve motivating the membership to engage in the goal-setting process. Most members are used to sitting back and letting the pastor and church officers tell them what the church is going to do (they are also used to letting leaders do the work). So it will be important to give them a new vision of their responsibility as members of Christ's body. The pastor might do it by a series of Sabbath sermons. Or perhaps the church might go on a weekend retreat with the expressed purpose of studying the church's mission.

In these meetings the pastor and those who assist him should lay a firm Biblical basis for mission. McGavran and Hunter suggest that we should not try to prompt by making people feel guilty for what they haven't done, but that motivation should rest upon the following four key elements:

1. Gratitude to Christ.
2. Obedience to the Great Commission.
3. Love for our neighbor.
4. Conviction that Christ is working with us.[5]

The preparatory work should include a study of the principles of church growth. On the retreat or at a meeting at the church, the congregation could view films on church growth. Study groups meeting weekly at the church or in private homes could go through this book or some other church growth manual and discuss the principles. The members should soon become excited about the prospects of getting involved in the process of charting the future of their beloved church.

Mission Statement

Now that the members are eager to do something, the next step may well be the writing of a mission statement. Such a statement is a brief but comprehensive formulation of what the church believes to be its unique purpose. Dean Hubbard has suggested that the mission statement should have as its basis (1) Biblical images and concepts, (2) theological and doctrinal concepts of church, (3) denominational tradition, (4) the needs of the world and contemporary society, (5) the local scene, and (6) the presence of the Holy Spirit.[6]

A mission statement is an overall philosophy that expresses the church's deeply held values. Hubbard says that if we start not with values but instead with existing programs, our goal statement may be just confirming the past. He proposes that our mission statement must:

1. Clearly identify the overall purpose of the church: whom we will minister to, how we will minister to them, and the results of our ministry.

2. Clearly indicate the general direction the church endeavors to move.

3. Clearly furnish a frame of reference for the relevancy of the church's goals.

4. Clearly set forth the emphasis, scope, and character of the church's programs.[7]

In preparation of the statement the membership must, first of all, receive some training in the composing of such documents. Then those willing to participate may divide into small groups of four to six members and write trial drafts. All of the drafts become the basic building material for the evangelism council or church board, which prepares the final statement. Then the council presents it to the full membership for their approval.

Following are two sample mission statements. Of course, an individual congregation would not simply copy another document, but would prepare one appropriate to its unique situation. We suggest that the statement may begin with descriptions appropriate to the church at large and then move to those aspects that correspond to its local mission.

70

A MODEL FOR CHURCH PLANNING

Statement of Mission

A statement of mission for the _____ church.

It is the purpose and mission of this church to witness to Jesus Christ as our Lord and Saviour; as a Christian church in our community to continue to find ways to share with our community the special message entrusted to us as Seventh-day Adventists; and to win as many to Christ and His message as God shall enable us to do.

It is our purpose that this church shall be a transforming fellowship in which the members can go on to maturity in Christ, and shall equip them for Christian service according to their gifts and abilities.

Because our church is part of a world movement, it shall be our purpose to reach out to the world, and to support our world mission through the organizations and institutions of the denomination of which we are a part.

Our Mission

We, the members of the _____ Seventh-day Adventist church, as part of the World Seventh-day Adventist organization, acknowledge our responsibility in fulfilling the commission given us by Christ to prepare the way for His second coming. To accomplish this, our mission is as follows:

1. To grow closer to Christ through personal Bible study, prayer, and individual commitment.

2. To uphold Christ before all within the church—adults, youth, and children—through worship, instruction, fellowship, and personal concern.

3. To present Christ to the people of _____ and the surrounding areas through community service and personal witness.

4. To carry Christ to the world field through prayer, financial contribution, and personal service.

The guide on the following page may aid the small groups in formulating the mission statement and the goals that spring from it.[8]

A PLANNING MODEL TO DEVELOP A MISSION STATEMENT

A Series of Sermons with Feedback-Discussion on the Nature of the Church and/or Special Study-Discussion Groups on the Same Subject

List the biblical images and theological concepts of the Church that are meaningful to you.	What world needs and issues should our church be concerned about today?	What needs and concerns of this community should our church be concerned about and doing something about?	What needs of church members should our church minister to?
Identify the four most important items with an *.	Identify the four most important items with an *.	Identify the four most important items with an *.	Identify the two most meaningful statements with an *.

EACH GROUP WRITES A
MISSION STATEMENT

ALL GROUPS COLLABORATE IN
WRITING A SINGLE CLEAR SPECIFIC
MISSION STATEMENT

ESTABLISH A PRIORITIZED
LIST OF CHURCH GOALS

DEVELOP A SERIES OF ACTION PLANS RESULTING FROM GOALS

IMPLEMENT AND EVALUATE THE ACTION PLAN

A MODEL FOR CHURCH PLANNING

Diagnostic Research

Between the writing of the mission statement and the setting of its goals, the church needs to do some serious study of both the congregation and the community. Virgil Gerber calls this diagnostic research. We have derived the following steps from his helpful manual:[9]

1. Compile the membership statistics of your church for the past ten years. They might include not only the actual totals in the membership records at the close of each calendar year but also any other valuable measures of growth available, such as church and Sabbath school attendance (although most churches don't bother, there is great value in keeping these kinds of records).

2. Plot the statistics on a bar or line graph. Prepare all graphs in large chart format or on overhead transparencies so that you can display them to the entire congregation.

3. Calculate the growth rates of your church for the entire ten-year-period and for each year within it. Plot them on separate graphs.

4. On the graph showing the actual growth rate for the previous ten years, plot another line for the biological growth rate. Experts generally estimate it at 25 percent per decade. Now it will be possible to compare how much better (or worse) your actual growth rate was than the one that would be assumed without any outreach.

5. Refine your data by breaking down the total figures into types of growth and losses—conversion, biological, transfer, kingdom, et cetera.

6. Analyze your growth patterns. Where did the new converts come from? Why was there a large transfer loss at some point? Did a good-sized group split off to plant a new church? Did an economic slump result in job losses with many moving to other communities in search of employment? Or was that the time the new pastor arrived? And what about that year with far-above-average growth? Was that when the conference sent in the big-name evangelist? Try to account for anything out of the usual.[10]

73

7. Do a thorough study of the local community—its resources, its demographic characteristics, its felt needs. It is such a large and important subject that we will devote a whole chapter to it ("Knowing Your Own Community"). In fact, it is the essential ingredient of the Caring Church.

8. Have one or more meetings with your entire church membership after the evangelism council or designated subcommittees have carried out the first seven steps. Now is the time to display all the charts, graphs, and analyses. Saturate the members with population facts about their community. Show them what is happening in their area and what God is doing in other similar areas. This will set the stage for the actual process of goal setting.

Set Goals

Goal setting comes after diagnostic research, for only in this sequence can one tie the goals to reality. Now that the members of the congregation have all the information, they should be able to set reasonable targets for baptisms, for church growth, and for other areas of their corporate life. Divide them into small task-force groups of six to eight members each. Ask each group to consider prayerfully all the evidence and then to make a projection for the next year and for four or five years into the future. Gerber suggests that (1) goals should be set in prayer, (2) goals should be established with a faith projection, realizing that God can multiply our resources, (3) goals must be realistic—not just wishful thinking but firmly undergirded by strategies and plans, and (4) the progress toward them should be evaluated annually, with new future projections as called for by the evidence.[11]

The evangelism council takes into consideration the reports of each subcommittee and then suggests the church goals. It presents them to the church board for approval, and finally the whole congregation votes on them. After a process like this, the goals are most likely to be appropriate for that church, and even more important, the members "own" them.

Write Objectives

While goals and objectives may seem to be similar, the

difference is basically one of detail. Objectives break down the overall goal into more manageable portions that one can evaluate more easily. The goal may be to baptize one hundred people next year, but the objectives state from what various sources those one hundred people will come. The larger goal may include many outcomes, but, according to Hubbard, the objective has one outcome, one or more processes, and a time frame.[12] Objectives also divide the goal chronologically into long-term, intermediate, and short-term steps. The writing of objectives follows the same process as that of goal setting. Done at the same time, it involves the same people. We describe it separately here only to emphasize the distinction between them and to point up the necessity for both.

Formulate Strategies

Strategies are the methods by which one reaches goals and objectives. They may include overall plans as well as detailed steps. For example, they may call for seed-sowing programs or "entry events" such as stress-control clinics, stop-smoking plans, or nutrition and cooking schools. Carefully drawn-up strategies may outline reaping methods such as evangelistic meetings or a revival series. They may propose dividing up the church's territory and assigning a section to each member[13] or other methods of mobilizing the laity. Or they may detail various ways of building lists of prospective converts and influencing the people on those lists.

The church may design strategies entirely at the local level, or it may borrow resources from the departments of the conference or from other sources and adapt them to the local situation. The important thing to remember is that goals and objectives are worthless without detailed and workable plans to make them reachable. The process of formulating plans and strategies should follow along the same lines as that of goal setting, with input from as many members of the congregation as possible and with the evangelism council or church board putting it all together. Of course, the full membership votes approval of the final document.

Design a Support System

So far, we have a wonderful plan. The problem is that in too many cases it remains just a *plan*. We once heard Charles Bradford, in his humorous style, remark that at our official church meetings we vote resolutions and speak of the process as *taking an action*. "Taking an action," he chuckled, "and we haven't even gotten it off the paper yet." If we don't want our plans to be just good reading material, we had better make sure that we set in motion the forces to carry them out.

This means that we (the evangelism council or church board) must assign the various tasks and delegate the authority necessary to perform them. We must provide the finances and a budget. The action steps are what *Dynamics of Church Growth* calls implementing. Hubbard suggests that we make a list of everything to be done and arrange it sequentially, then set the tasks up in a time-frame chart, with each item to be completed by a certain date. Individuals should report at regular intervals to the council on the progress and eventually on the completion of their assignments.[14]

Evaluate the Plan

At stated intervals we need to evaluate the various plans to see whether the church is reaching its goals. This is the final step in the *Dynamics of Church Growth* plan. The church can then make adjustments to keep the whole program on course. Experience may reveal it wise to modify the goals or objectives, the strategies, or the support system.

Church growth does not just happen. A congregation that wishes to grow must plan to grow. Through its representative committees, the whole church becomes involved and has input. First, the church prepares a mission statement. In line with what the *church* has accepted as its mission, it formulates written goals that outline long-term, intermediate, and short-term objectives toward fulfilling that mission. Then the church devises methods and strategies to accomplish those objectives, and implements them. Under the guidance of the Holy Spirit this is the portrait of a growing church.

A MODEL FOR CHURCH PLANNING

References

[1] Roger Dudley, Des Cummings, Mary Lou Cummings, and Greg Clark. "Church Growth in Washington," pp. 20, 22, 24-26, 28, 29.

[2] Dudley and Cummings, "Church Growth in NAD," pp. 64, 70, 71, 74, 84.

[3] Clark, Dudley, and Cummings, "Church Growth in Hawaii," pp. 16, 17, 19, 21-23, 26, 27.

[4] North American Division of Seventh-day Adventists, *Dynamics of Church Growth* (Washington, D.C.: NAD, 1982).

[5] Donald McGavran and George G. Hunter, III, *Church Growth: Strategies That Work* (Nashville: Abingdon, 1980), pp. 72, 73.

[6] Dean Hubbard, series of lectures presented at Columbia Union Conference Church Growth Conference, Takoma Park, Maryland, January 14-16, 1980.

[7] *Ibid.*

[8] Adapted from Alvin J. Lindgren and Norman Shawchuck, *Management for Your Church* (Nashville: Abingdon, 1977).

[9] Virgil Gerber, *God's Way to Keep a Church Going and Growing* (Glendale, Calif.: Regal Books, 1973), pp. 33-36, 47-62.

[10] Other valuable ways of analyzing your church will be discussed more fully in the chapters "Making the Most of a Profile" and "Whom Are We Winning?"

[11] Gerber, *op. cit.,* pp. 62-66.

[12] Hubbard, *op. cit.*

[13] For a detailed description of territorial assignment, see George E. Knowles, *How to Help Your Church Grow* (Washington, D.C.: Review and Herald Pub. Assn., 1981), pp. 63-80.

[14] *Ibid.*

8

Knowing Your Own Community

Have you heard about the drunk who lost his wallet in a dark alley but went looking for it under the corner lamppost because the light was better there? Sometimes we are like that in our evangelistic approaches. We offer the public what *we* think they need, rather than what *they* think they need. We give them "what is good for them," rather than what they are prepared to accept. This leads to the concept of "felt needs."

All people have certain problems and concerns that currently dominate their lives. They also have needs of which they may not be aware—for example, the lack of God in their lives. While these latter needs may be vitally important, it is often difficult to appeal to them, because of the more pressing felt needs. A man who hasn't eaten in two days will probably have no interest in a lecture on the prophecies.

Therefore, to reach the people around us successfully, we must discover their immediate concerns. Perhaps they worry about their jobs, their health, or their families. These suggest the avenues by which we can best approach them. The apostle Paul employed this method:

> To the Jews I became like a Jew, to win the Jews. To those

under the law I became like one under the law (though I myself am not under the law), so as to win those under the law. To those not having the law I became like one not having the law (though I am not free from God's law but am under Christ's law), so as to win those not having the law. To the weak I became weak, to win the weak. I have become all things to all men so that by all possible means I might save some (1 Cor. 9:20-22).

In modern times, Robert Schuller concisely expressed the idea when he said that the secret of church growth is to find a need and meet it. It also seems to appear in Ellen White's description of Christ's manner of dealing with people.

Christ's method alone will give true success in reaching the people. The Saviour mingled with men as one who desired their good. He showed His sympathy for them, ministered to their needs, and won their confidence. Then He bade them, "Follow Me." [1]

Approaching people on the level of their felt needs is at the very core of the Caring Church model.

Using a Community Survey

One way to discover the felt needs of a community is to ask the people. You may do it by means of a community survey. Such a survey should have several characteristics:

1. It must be short and simple. People are busy. If you want them to cooperate, you must be able to assure them that it will take only a minute or two.

2. It should move from the more pressing personal concerns in a logical flow that finally touches gently on spiritual issues.

3. It should be a genuine effort to listen to the community, rather than to tell them something. Sometimes we have approached homes with what purported to be a survey, but which was actually an attempt to begin Bible studies. Not only does it make the people feel as if we have deceived them, but it deprives the church of the benefits of really knowing what the community is thinking. We will have plenty of time to offer our services later. At this point we should *listen.*

The Institute of Church Ministry in consultation with James Engel, of the school of communications at Wheaton

College, has designed a simple survey, which we include here. In constructing it, we studied a national poll on the problems that people feel most concerned about, and then tried to incorporate them into our survey. We are not suggesting that it is the right survey for every community, but it does attempt to illustrate the principles described above. Short and administered quickly, it begins with common concerns like finances, job, and health, and then moves into more emotional and subjective areas like stress, marriage, and children. Then it touches on the spiritual and philosophical realms with questions 11 and 12, and finally asks directly about relationship to God.

Such a survey we can take at the front door or over the telephone. Church members may be happy to volunteer for knocking or calling when they find they are free to listen and are not under pressure to wring a commitment out of the respondents. If an area is too heavily populated to cover every home, one can approximate a random selection by choosing every fifth (or other number) home or name in the telephone directory.

The survey taker introduces himself/herself at the door or over the phone and says something like: "I represent the Seventh-day Adventist Community Services, and we are taking a brief survey to discover the major concerns of people in this community. It takes only about a minute. May I ask you a few quick questions?" If the resident is agreeable, the survey taker turns so they can both see the questionnaire on top of a pad or clipboard and reads the instructions aloud. Then he/she asks each question and circles the number the respondent chooses. Wrap up the session with something like: "Thank you very much for your help. We are going to be designing some special seminars to meet those concerns that most people choose. We'll be announcing these to the community, so keep a lookout for them. Would you like to be informed of programs that would relate to your interests?"

COMMUNITY FELT NEEDS SURVEY

Everybody has some concerns or even worries. Below is a list of things that some Americans are concerned about. Please rate each one as a *concern for you* like this:

Circle the number that shows your degree of concern:

No Concern / Some Concern / Quite a Bit of Concern / A Great Deal of Concern

1. Finances—making a decent living 1 2 3 4
2. Being successful on my job 1 2 3 4
3. Having good health 1 2 3 4
4. Smoking too much 1 2 3 4
5. My weight 1 2 3 4
6. Time pressures—getting everything done. 1 2 3 4
7. Stress—being uptight 1 2 3 4
8. Quality of my marriage 1 2 3 4
9. Bringing up my children right 1 2 3 4
10. Peace of mind 1 2 3 4
11. Understanding the meaning of life 1 2 3 4
12. My relationship with God 1 2 3 4

City_____ Area_____
Male or Female_____ Approximate Age_____

The information at the bottom of the sheet does not come directly from the respondent, but the survey taker fills it in after leaving the home. It is important to indicate clearly the area (unless it is a small town), because some parts of the city may have different concerns than others. And the ability to distinguish between the needs of various subpopulations and therefore to use different approaches lies at the heart of knowing your community.

Demographic Studies

Asking the people is one way to learn about a community and its needs. Another method is to build a community profile based on demographic information. A number of local sources offer such data: the chamber of commerce, the city or regional planning commission, the Ministerial Association, and insurance companies, for instance. But the most comprehensive information for major cities comes from the United States Census Bureau and is available from them or in libraries. Building a useful profile from such a massive amount of data, however, is a formidable task when done by hand, and many churches or groups of churches in a single area prefer a computer analysis.

The Institute of Church Ministry has joined with an interdenominational consortium to make computer profiles of selected areas available at a reasonable cost.[2] The model that the group has chosen is called "Long Community Profile—Summary Tape File 1," and we have illustrated it here. The profile has twenty-four modules with a total of eighty-five pieces of information. All information is given for each census tract.

In theory a census tract is an area of the city that contains about four thousand people. In practice these numbers fluctuate with the growth and decline of the population. In the 1980 census, for example, the four counties that comprised Greater Atlanta, Georgia, averaged about 5,700 people per tract, with considerable variation.

On the profile the county (identified by number) appears in column 1. Column 2 contains the particular tract number. In order to interpret the profile, the reader must have access to a census map of the area that prints the tract numbers in their proper location. The profile lists the information called for in module 1 for each census tract in the area requested in numerical order. Then it goes back over the same tracts with the data in module 2, and so on. The first twelve modules give information as actual numbers of people. Modules 13 to 24 repeat the data of modules 1 to 12, but provide the information as percentages of the total. In areas of many census tracts (Greater Atlanta has 265), the computer printout may run to a very thick document indeed.

1980 Census Data
Long Community Profile—STF 1

#1 General Population Characteristics

1	2	3	4	5	6	7
county	tract	total population	urbanized population	rural population	male population	female population

#2 Family (Related) Households

1	2	3	4	5	6	7	8	9
county	tract	total households family	married couples	male family	female family	married couple child	male family child	female family child

#3 Non-family Households

1	2	3	4	5	6	7	8	9
county	tract	total households non-family male	one person male	one person female	two or more male head	two or more female head	inmates	other persons/group qtr.

#4 Marital Status—Persons

1	2	3	4	5	6	7	8
county	tract	total persons (status)	single	married except (separated)	separated	widowed	divorced

#5 Race—Module 1

1	2	3	4	5	6	7	8	9	10
county	tract	total persons	white	black	Asian Indian	Korean	Vietnamese	Japanese	Chinese

#6 Race—Module 2

1	2	3	4	5	6	7	8	9	10
county	tract	Native	Eskimo	Aleut	Hawaiian	Guamanian	S...		

1	2	3	4	5	6	7	8	9	10
county	tract	total Spanish	Mexican origin	Puerto Rican origin	Cuban origin	other Spanish origin	White Spanish	Black Spanish	other races Spanish

#8 Age Structure—Module 1

1	2	3	4	5	6	7	8	9	10
county	tract	median age	median male	median female	persons < 6	persons 6-9	persons 10-14	persons 15-17	persons 18-24

#9 Age Structure—Module 2

1	2	3	4	5	6	7	8
county	tract	persons 25-34	persons 35-44	persons 45-54	persons 55-64	persons 65-74	persons 75 +

#10 General Housing Characteristics

1	2	3	4	5	6	7	8	9	10
county	tract	total units	owner occupied	renter occupied	vac./for sale/rent	vacant seasonal	vacant yr. round	total condo	mobile home

#11 Housing Structure

1	2	3	4	5	6	7	8
county	tract	one unit at address	2-9 units at address	10 + units at address	median number rooms	median persons/ room	units lacking plumbing

#12 Housing Value

1	2	3	4	5	6	7	8	9	10
county	tract	median value	median valued < $10,000	median valued < $20,000	median valued > $100,000	median valued > $200,000	median rent	median rent < $100	median rent > $500

In addition to this basic profile, a church can secure one that gives all the information for the present census, then lists the same information for the previous census and calculates the numerical and percentage change. Thus we can note the amount and direction of change for each census tract on each item between 1970 and 1980. Though somewhat more expensive than the basic profile, it provides valuable data on what is happening to communities. It is also possible to secure computer-drawn population pyramids that graphically display the age and sex characteristics of each census tract by race for both the current and previous censuses.

Target Populations

Having collected a wide variety of information about your community through surveys and demographic studies, the next task is to pinpoint specific groups that will have distinctive needs and interests. The groups may be divisions of the demographic variables, such as race, marital status, age, level of income, or type of housing. Or they may be people with common concerns as revealed by the community survey. We call them target populations.

In our evangelistic approaches we have often used the "shotgun" method and directed the same appeal to everyone in town. Not only is this method wasteful, but it fails to attract many people who might have responded if the approach had touched upon their particular concerns. Focusing on the concrete needs of one or more target populations within the community will be more productive and efficient.

The demographic studies based on U.S. Census information allow church growth planners to determine the characteristic features of the people who live within a given census tract. For example, the dominant racial group may shape the type of appeal. Or a high percentage of married people with preschool children or a heavy concentration of teen-agers may suggest an approach. Since church growth studies have shown that recently mobile people are more open to new ideas than those who have lived in the same place over a period of time, areas that indicate rapid increase in the population stand out as prime evangelistic targets.

At this point, by combining the demographic data with the information from the community survey, it will be possible to assign felt needs to the various target populations and begin to do some brainstorming about possible programs that might address them. An excellent workbook to help a church organize this process is *Church Growth Plans: A Planning Guide*, produced by the Northern California Conference.[3]

Entry Events

Entry events, in the Caring Church model, are those programs or services through which nonmembers first participate in a church-sponsored activity. They may range from the specifically doctrinal to the nonreligious, depending upon the felt needs of the target population. For example, a series of Bible lectures entitled "What Seventh-day Adventists Believe" might be an entry event for some people who were actively searching for a church right for them. But for most people that would not have suitable appeal. Something with a general spiritual theme might do for the religiously inclined. Most entry events, however, will have to speak to the concerns of the "secular" mind.

By meeting people on the level of their felt needs, even when they appear to have little relation to religion, the church has opportunity to demonstrate love and caring. People establish a contact with the church and take the initiative to come to an event it conducts. They have overcome barriers of uncertainty, suspicion, and apathy. The way opens for them to become more fully involved in the life of the church and eventually walk down the path to full membership.

A study of the felt needs of target populations will suggest possible entry events. Since health concerns rate high for many people, some churches have planned entry events such as Five-Day Plans to Stop Smoking, alcohol- and/or drug-abuse seminars, cooking and nutrition schools, weight-control clinics, stress-management seminars, and vegetarian restaurants.

Other events may focus on family issues. Examples are premarriage forums, marriage enrichment seminars, workshops on communication skills and conflict management, parenting skills, working mothers' seminars, and managing family finances.

Then some events cater to the needs of special groups: Vacation Bible Schools, Pathfinders, senior citizens, a job-counseling service, a seminar in study skills, child-care services, the Community Services center, and a seminar on grief, death, and dying.

Some churches have had good success with cultural programs, such as a Sacred Artist Music Series. For those with felt spiritual needs, a Daniel seminar or a Life in the Spirit seminar might be appropriate. Concerned Communications offers complete instructions and all necessary materials for conducting a number of entry-event seminars.[4]

The crucial element in this planning is, of course, to be sure that the church schedules all entry events in response to felt needs that it has identified in that particular community for a special target population. The caring church always puts people ahead of programs.

Pathways to the Church

To conduct entry events without follow-up is equivalent to a fisherman throwing his bait into the water without having it attached to a hook and a line. Not that the church should condition its loving ministry upon having its recipients accept its unique teachings and request membership. But Seventh-day Adventists believe that a complete helping ministry involves leading people to know Jesus Christ, accept His offer of salvation, and become part of His body.

Therefore the church should carefully compile a prospect list from those who attend entry events. If each year the number of people participating in one or more entry events would equal the size of the congregation's membership, the church would soon have a substantial list of individuals who have indicated an interest in what it has to offer. Carefully cultivated, the list should result in significant additions to the church.

But people do not usually decide to join the church as a result of their first contact with it. They must have repeated involvement. The church will plan a program for each prospect that may lead him/her from the entry event into full membership. This takes place gradually over a period of time. We may think of the sequence of experiences as a pathway into the church. It leads the individual from the satisfaction of one felt need to another. The pathway often progresses from the "secular" needs to the more spiritual concerns and finally to the unique message Adventists proclaim. What may be an entry event for one person may be a station farther down the road for another, and vice versa. The pathway is specific to each individual, but a successful one will always lead to a commitment to Christ and the church.

Wherever the pathways begin, they finally bring the person through areas of the religious life with programs like the various Bible study programs, home Bible fellowships, pastor's Bible classes, public evangelistic meetings, Daniel or Revelation seminars, and baptismal classes. Finally he or she makes a decision for Jesus Christ and His church, and the congregation keeps growing. The concept "The Caring Church" sums it all up.

Someone has said, "You can't love me if you don't know me." The church cannot share the love of God with a community it does not know. If our church is to make an impact and achieve conversion growth, it must study its community and know its needs. Then it must do something about those needs. Remember: "The secret of church growth is to find a need and meet it."

References

[1] Ellen G. White, *The Ministry of Healing* (Mountain View, Calif.: Pacific Press Pub. Assn., 1905), p. 143.

[2] For estimates, write to the Institute of Church Ministry, Andrews University, Berrien Springs, Michigan 49104. If possible, enclose a census map and specify the tract numbers. Otherwise include a large city map with the desired areas marked by colored line.

[3] Write to the Ministerial Department of the Northern California Conference, P.O. Box 23165, Pleasant Hill, California 94523.

[4] Concerned Communications, P.O. Box 700, Arroyo Grande, California 93420.

9

Making the Most of a Profile

In the chapter "A Model for Church Planning" we included a section on "Diagnostic Research." There we suggested that before setting church growth goals, we do some serious research of both the church and the community. The chapter just before this one concentrated on examining the local community, and earlier in this book we gave some information about one specific way that we can follow as we seek to study the local church—by analyzing growth trends over a ten-year period.

This chapter explains another helpful method of examining a local congregation—that of surveying the membership to determine the attitudes and behaviors present that may point either to a vital, growing church, or a stagnating one, likely to decline. To aid in this task, the Institute of Church Ministry has developed a questionnaire that in one form or another we have used in our division-wide project or in a number of conferences to collect data on thousands of Adventist members. It is now known as the "Caring Church Survey." We exhibit a copy of the questionnaire here.

INSTRUCTIONS FOR ADMINISTERING
THE CARING CHURCH SURVEY
FROM THE
INSTITUTE OF CHURCH MINISTRY

Church _____

Code No. _____ No. Surveys_____

If you are the pastor of a church in which the membership is being surveyed using the PRE-EVANGELISM INVENTORY, here is everything you need to know to do the job. It will not take a great deal of your precious time, but it is important to follow directions.

The plan is to conduct the survey during a Sabbath service, asking the baptized members present to complete it. We suggest using the lay activities period but lengthening it to about twenty to twenty-five minutes. Most people will complete the survey in fifteen minutes or less which will allow time for explanations and for distributing and collecting the material. If you prefer a different time during the Sabbath services, fine. The main thing is to survey as far as possible all members present on a given Sabbath.

Spiritual Emphasis

Some will question whether this is appropriate on the Sabbath. We believe this depends on the way it is handled. We urge you to take a brief period (perhaps five minutes) to talk about the survey in the light of finishing God's work. Tell the congregation that your local and conference leaders are deeply concerned about the fulfillment of the Great Commission. They need to find out why we have or have not been successful in soul winning and what can be done about it. Tell them that this is an opportunity to take spiritual inventory of how they see themselves and their church. This information will help the pastors and the conference leaders to give wiser direction to God's cause in their districts and throughout all the conference. Tell them that the questions can help focus on areas in their own lives that need changing and may thus prove to be a positive spiritual experience. Mention that results of the survey will be used in planning a soul-winning thrust in the community.

Specific Instructions

1. Tell the members a week ahead of time so they will be mentally prepared. Don't just drop it on them. You might mention that your church has been chosen for an important study that will help your conference leaders lay plans for finishing the work. Tell them that a special time schedule will be arranged for next Sabbath.

2. Bring extra pencils for those who have forgotten a writing implement. Pens are OK.

3. Give the survey only to baptized members of this local church.

4. We have estimated by a formula the number of surveys you will need. In a few churches there might not be enough to cover everyone. Don't worry. Just give them out as far as they go.

5. Emphasize that there are *no right answers*. We need to know how the members actually believe and do, not how they think they should answer the questions.

6. Ask them to circle a *number*—not a word—for each question.

7. If a member has difficulty in choosing a response or feels that none of the choices is exactly applicable, instruct him to pick the choice nearest to what he feels is right, but to *answer every question*. Blanks in the data throw off the results.

8. Instruct members to make their answers reflect *habitual attitudes and practices over the past year* rather than the present state of affairs.

9. Emphasize that all answers are confidential. Members do not put their names on the sheets and no one will know how they answered. The number on the survey is a church code and is the *same for everyone* in their church.

After the members are finished, collect the surveys and early the next week return them to the designated place.

Do not return unused surveys since they are coded for your church. A profile will be provided showing the percentage of the members who chose each response.

Thanks for your help. Blessings on you in your ministry.

Caring Church Survey

1. CIRCLE THE <u>NUMBER</u> SHOWING HOW LONG
   YOU HAVE BEEN A BAPTIZED ADVENTIST.

   1. LESS THAN 1 YEAR
   2. 1-5 YEARS
   3. 6-10 YEARS
   4. 11-20 YEARS
   5. OVER 20 YEARS

2. WAS AT LEAST ONE OF YOUR PARENTS AN
   ADVENTIST SOMETIME DURING THE FIRST
   12 YEARS OF YOUR LIFE?

   1. YES   2. NO

3. CIRCLE THE <u>NUMBER</u> INDICATING THE
   RELATIONSHIP THAT YOU HAVE WITH
   JESUS CHRIST.

   NONE   INTIMATE
   1   2   3   4   5

4. WHAT <u>NUMBER</u> SHOWS YOUR ASSURANCE
   THAT YOU HAVE ETERNAL LIFE?

   NOT SURE   VERY CERTAIN
   1   2   3   4   5

5. TO WHAT EXTENT HAVE YOU ATTENDED
   ADVENTIST SCHOOLS?

   NOT AT   ALL THE
   ALL   WAY

   A) ELEMENTARY   1   2   3   4   5

   B) ACADEMY   1   2   3   4   5

   C) COLLEGE   1   2   3   4   5

6. CIRCLE THE <u>NUMBER</u> WHICH SHOWS THE
   EMPHASIS YOUR PASTOR PLACES ON
   SOUL-WINNING.

   LITTLE   TOP
   IMPORTANCE   PRIORITY
   1   2   3   4   5

7. HOW DO YOU FEEL ABOUT THE MONEY
   THE CONFERENCE SPENDS ON PUBLIC
   EVANGELISM? CIRCLE A <u>NUMBER</u>.

   TOO MUCH   SHOULD
   SPENT   SPEND MORE
   1   2   3   4   5

8. HOW WELL PREPARED ARE YOU FOR THE
   WORK OF SOUL-WINNING? CIRCLE A
   <u>NUMBER</u>.

   NOT AT ALL   VERY WELL
   1   2   3   4   5

9. HAVE YOU BEEN ENGAGED IN SOME
   TYPE OF SOUL-WINNING OVER THE
   PAST YEAR?.

   1. YES   2. NO

Institute of Church Ministry, 1982

		YES	NO
10.	DO YOU HOLD A CHURCH OFFICE OR OTHER SERVICE POSITION?	1	2
11.	DID YOU SET A PERSONAL SOUL-WINNING GOAL THIS YEAR?	1	2
12.	HAVE YOU BEEN INVOLVED IN COMMUNITY OUTREACH SERVICES (Dorcas, Stop Smoking, Etc.)?	1	2
13.	HAVE YOU HELD BIBLE STUDIES WITH A NON-ADVENTIST THIS YEAR?	1	2
14.	WITHIN THE LAST YEAR HAVE YOU ATTENDED A WITNESSING TRAINING PROGRAM?	1	2

15. HOW MUCH DO YOU AGREE WITH THESE STATEMENTS? CIRCLE THE NUMBER.

	DISAGREE STRONGLY				AGREE STRONGLY
A) MY FAMILY HELPS MY RELATION-SHIP WITH CHRIST.	1	2	3	4	5
B) I WOULD FEEL COMFORTABLE BRINGING A VISITOR TO OUR SABBATH SCHOOL.	1	2	3	4	5
C) MOST SABBATH SERMONS ARE QUITE INTERESTING.	1	2	3	4	5
D) WE HAVE GENERALLY HAD GOOD EXPERIENCE WITH PUBLIC EVANGELISM IN THIS CHURCH.	1	2	3	4	5
E) OUR CHURCH SHOULD JOIN WITH OTHER ADVENTIST CHURCHES TO HOLD CRUSADES.	1	2	3	4	5
F) PEOPLE WHO ARE BROUGHT INTO THE CHURCH IN EVANGELISTIC MEETINGS JUST DO NOT STAY.	1	2	3	4	5
G) I CAN SPEAK EASILY ABOUT MY FAITH.	1	2	3	4	5
H) THE BIBLE IS DULL AND DOES NOT HELP ME IN LIFE.	1	2	3	4	5

16. HOW MANY PEOPLE HAVE YOU BEEN WHOLLY OR PARTIALLY RESPONSIBLE FOR BRINGING INTO THE CHURCH IN THE LAST THREE YEARS?

1. UNAWARE OF ANY
2. ONE
3. TWO TO FIVE
4. SIX TO TEN
5. MORE THAN TEN

17. CIRCLE THE NUMBER WHICH SHOWS
THE DEGREE THAT YOU HAVE BEEN
INVOLVED IN:

		DOESN'T APPLY	NEVER	SOMETIMES	USUALLY	ALWAYS
A)	DAILY PERSONAL BIBLE STUDY	1	2	3	4	5
B)	DAILY PRAYER FOR THE CONVERSION OF SPECIFIC PEOPLE	1	2	3	4	5
C)	REGULAR STUDY OF ELLEN WHITE BOOKS	1	2	3	4	5
D)	REGULAR FINANCIAL SUPPORT FOR LOCAL SOUL-WINNING	1	2	3	4	5
E)	MEET REGULARLY WITH A SMALL STUDY OR FELLOWSHIP GROUP	1	2	3	4	5
F)	HELP NEIGHBORS WITH THEIR PERSONAL PROBLEMS	1	2	3	4	5
G)	CONCERN FOR THOSE WHO HAVE NOT ACCEPTED CHRIST	1	2	3	4	5
H)	DAILY FAMILY WORSHIP	1	2	3	4	5
I)	WITNESSING IN EVERYDAY ACTIVITIES	1	2	3	4	5
J)	ATTENDING SABBATH SCHOOL	1	2	3	4	5
K)	TITHING	1	2	3	4	5
L)	WORKING TO WIN NON-ADVENTIST RELATIVES	1	2	3	4	5

18. CIRCLE THE NUMBER WHICH BEST
DESCRIBES YOUR CHURCH GROUP:

A)   1   2   3   4   5
NOT A SOUL-   SOUL-WINNING
WINNING CHURCH   CHURCH

B)   1   2   3   4   5
LOW ADVENTIST   HIGH ADVENTIST
STANDARDS   STANDARDS

C)   1   2   3   4   5
COLD AND   WARM AND
UNFRIENDLY   FRIENDLY

D)   1   2   3   4   5
NEW MEMBERS   NEW MEMBERS
IGNORED   INVOLVED IN
                     FELLOWSHIP &
                     ACTIVITIES

E)   1   2   3   4   5
I DON'T SEEM   MY KIND OF
TO FIT IN   PEOPLE

4

19. HOW MANY OF YOUR CLOSE FRIENDS
    ARE NON-ADVENTISTS?   1   2   3   4   5
                                          NONE   MANY

20. CIRCLE THE NUMBER OF THE AGE
    GROUP YOU ARE IN.   1. 19 YEARS OR UNDER
                                           2. 20-35 YEARS
                                           3. 36-50 YEARS
                                           4. 51-65 YEARS
                                           5. OVER 65 YEARS

21. CIRCLE THE NUMBER WHICH SHOWS
    YOUR YEARLY FAMILY INCOME.   1. UNDER $8,000
                                           2. $8,001 TO $16,000
                                           3. $16,001 TO $25,000
                                           4. $25,001 TO $50,000
                                           5. OVER $50,000

22. CIRCLE THE NUMBER THAT SHOWS
    YOUR ETHNIC BACKGROUND.   1. WHITE
                                           2. SPANISH
                                           3. BLACK
                                           4. ASIAN
                                           5. OTHER

23. CIRCLE THE NUMBER THAT SHOWS
    THE DISTANCE THAT YOU LIVE
    FROM THE CHURCH.   1. UNDER 3 MILES
                                           2. 4-10 MILES
                                           3. 11-15 MILES
                                           4. 16-25 MILES
                                           5. OVER 25 MILES

24. YOUR SEX.   1. MALE
                                           2. FEMALE

PLEASE ANSWER ALL QUESTIONS.

THANK YOU FOR YOUR COOPERATION.

AICG-7

In explaining how to obtain maximum benefit from the survey, this chapter adopts the model of a church growth consultant or "pastor developer" who works with the pastor and local congregational leaders to interpret the survey results and plan appropriate strategies based upon them. This developer might be the conference ministerial director, another experienced pastor, or a professional church planner employed for the purpose. If no such individual exists, the pastor may still utilize the procedures described in this chapter in working with his local leaders to develop a plan for church growth.

Generating a Church Profile

When a church seeks to utilize the consulting services of a developer, it is paramount that the latter have access to information that will help him to be specific in his task of diagnosing strengths and weaknesses. One aspect is the completion, by all attending members on a particular Sabbath, of the Caring Church Survey. The local congregation should fill it out either at the beginning or end of the worship service. We have included a copy of the instructions for administering the survey along with a suggested spiritual emphasis approach.

Administer the survey at least six weeks prior to the date that the developer plans to meet with the pastor. This will allow time for the surveys to come to ICM, be entered into the computer, a profile generated, and copies of the profile sent to both the developer and the pastor. The computer-generated profile prints out each question from the survey and shows the percentage of the respondents who selected each answer choice. A sample profile from "Anytown" appears on pages 100 and 101.

Individual Survey Analysis

When the developer receives his copy of the church profile, he should begin to analyze the strengths and weaknesses of the congregation that he is going to assist. Second, he should send a letter instructing the pastor regarding: (a) a method of investigating his church's needs and strengths; (b) the time and date for their consultation appointment. It might resemble the following sample:

Dear————:

Today I received a profile of your church from the Institute of Church Ministry at Andrews University. I am giving it careful consideration so that I can understand the unique strengths and weaknesses of the congregation in which you minister [if this is more than a one-church district, use the plural, "congregations in which you minister"]. Let me share with you how I am approaching the task of understanding your church so you can follow a similar format that will allow us to compare our conclusions. I am going through the church profile and beside each question that I feel displays a particular strength, I am placing a plus (+). Beside those that appear to portray a particular weakness, I am putting a minus (−). Questions that need further investigation or are somewhat confusing will receive a question mark (?). After evaluating each question in this manner, I am assembling a list of strengths and weaknesses that the survey has revealed. I do not feel that the survey is infallible; therefore, I am asking you to identify any questions in which you feel the profile does not fairly represent your church. As we review the strengths and weaknesses of your congregation our purpose will be to establish a leadership agenda ranked according to priority. If you have the opportunity to set down what you feel are the most important things we must deal with, it will be a real bonus. However, I would like to request that you at least complete the process of listing the church's strengths and weaknesses. I am planning on being with you and your evangelism council on [insert date] beginning at [insert time], and have set aside [insert number of hours] for this meeting. I would like to request that we would be able to do this in a quiet environment where we will not be interrupted. I have asked my secretary not to call or give out the number of the church unless it is a dire emergency. In the meantime, I will be praying that God will provide us special insights into your congregation so we can work together in developing an effective church growth strategy.

(Signature)

CHURCH GROWTH SURVEY—INSTITUTE OF CHURCH MINISTRY

Theological Seminary, Andrews University

Church
ANY TOWN

Number of surveys for this report = 109

1. Circle the number showing how long you have been a baptized Adventist.

Less than 1 year	1-5 years	6-10 years	11-20 years	Over 20 years
6%	14%	10%	20%	50%

2. Was at least one of your parents an Adventist sometime during the first 12 years of your life?

Yes	No
67%	33%

3. Circle the number indicating the relationship that you have with Jesus Christ.

None 1	2	3	4	5 Intimate
1%	9%	37%	27%	27%

4. What number shows your assurance that you have eternal life?

Not sure 1	2	3	4	5 Very certain
5%	10%	24%	25%	37%

5. To what extent have you attended Adventist schools?

	Not at all 1	2	3	4	5 All the way
A) Elementary	51%	4%	12%	4%	29%
B) Academy	45%	3%	9%	6%	37%
C) College	46%	12%	11%	7%	24%

6. Circle the number which shows the emphasis your pastor places on soul-winning.

Little importance 1	2	3	4	5 Top priority
2%	4%	26%	42%	27%

7. How do you feel about the money the conference spends on public evangelism? Circle a number.

Too much spent 1	2	3	4	5 Should spend more
5%	7%	49%	21%	18%

8. How well prepared are you for the work of soul-winning? Circle a number.

Not at all 1	2	3	4	5 Very well
19%	36%	34%	7%	4%

9. Have you been engaged in some type of soul-winning over the past year?

Yes	No
46%	54%

10. Do you hold a church office or other service position? 57% / 43%
11. Did you set a personal soul-winning goal this year? 15% / 85%
12. Have you been involved in community outreach services (Dorcas, Stop Smoking, etc.)? 39% / 61%
13. Have you held Bible studies with a non-Adventist this year? 13% / 87%
14. Within the last year have you attended a witnessing training program? 7% / 93%

15. How much do you agree with these statements?

	Disagree strongly 1	2	3	4	5 Agree strongly
A) My family helps my relationship with Christ.	4%	5%	30%	22%	39%
B) I would feel comfortable bringing a visitor to Sabbath school.					
C) Most Sabbath sermons are quite interesting.	2%	10%	18%	25%	45%
D) We have generally had good experience with public evangelism in this church.	6%	11%	28%	28%	28%
E) Our church should join with other Adventist churches to hold crusades.	6%	17%	44%	22%	11%
F) People who are brought into the church in evangelistic meetings do not stay.	7%	5%	40%	24%	24%
G) I can speak easily about my faith.	7%	20%	43%	22%	7%
H) The Bible is dull and does not help me in life.	4%	16%	30%	29%	21%

16. How many people have you been wholly or partially responsible for bringing into the church in the last three years?

Unaware of any	One	2-5	6-10	More than 10
72%	15%	11%	2%	1%

17. Circle the number which shows the degree that you have been involved in:

DA—Doesn't apply
N —Never
S —Sometimes
U —Usually
A —Always

	DA	N	S	U	A
A) Daily personal Bible study	1%	5%	38%	39%	17%
B) Daily prayer for the conversion of specific people	3%	12%	32%	23%	30%
C) Regular study of Ellen White books	6%	12%	61%	12%	9%
D) Regular financial support for local soul-winning	6%	12%	39%	17%	26%
E) Meet regularly with a small study or fellowship group	9%	42%	32%	8%	8%
F) Help neighbors with their personal problems	7%	8%	50%	24%	11%
G) Concern for those who have not accepted Christ	2%	4%	32%	29%	33%
H) Daily family worship	7%	11%	28%	25%	29%
I) Witnessing in everyday activities	3%	6%	47%	29%	15%
J) Attending Sabbath school	1%	4%	4%	23%	69%
K) Tithing	0%	1%	10%	9%	80%
L) Working to win non-Adventist relatives	7%	17%	31%	25%	20%

18. Circle the number which best describes your church group:

A) Soul-winning church	No	1 2%	2 7%	3 49%	4 30%	5 12%	Yes
B) Adventist standards	Low	1 4%	2 3%	3 27%	4 41%	5 26%	High
C) Friendliness	Cold and unfriendly	1 3%	2 8%	3 31%	4 23%	5 35%	Warm and friendly
D) New members	Ignored	1 5%	2 15%	3 30%	4 30%	5 20%	Involved
E) Feelings toward church people	I don't fit in	1 5%	2 5%	3 32%	4 29%	5 29%	My kind of people

19. How many of your close friends are non-Adventists?

None	1	2	3	4	5	Many
14%	28%	24%	12%	21%		

20. Circle the number of the age group you are in.

19 years or under	20-35 years	36-50 years	51-65 years	Over 65 years
10%	37%	27%	20%	6%

21. Circle the number which shows your yearly family income.

Under $8,000	$8,001-$16,000	$16,001-$25,000	$25,001-$50,000	Above $50,000
9%	11%	25%	55%	0%

22. Circle the number that shows your ethnic background.

White	Spanish	Black	Asian	Other
95%	3%	0%	0%	2%

33. Circle the number that shows the distance that you live from the church.

Under 3 miles	4-10 miles	11-15 miles	16-25 miles	Over 25 miles
34%	60%	4%	2%	0%

24. Your sex.

Male	Female
46%	54%

This letter should go out at least two weeks before the consultation date. The developer should spend time in personal prayer holding up the name of the pastor, praying that God will create an open and Spirit-filled atmosphere in which growth can take place.

The Consultation

Armed with the power of prayer and the church profile, the developer is ready for a face-to-face working session with the pastor and his local leaders. As the session begins he should spend the first few minutes in outlining the procedure of consultation. He might say something like "I am really excited about the opportunity to work together today. Let me just share with you what we will seek to accomplish during our time together.

"1. We need to spend time together in prayer.

"2. I want to check my perceptions with the pastor's regarding the strengths and weaknesses of the congregation.

"3. I'd like to have us work on an agenda of needs in the church.

"4. After ranking the needs, we will discuss resources and strategies for meeting them.

"5. We should prepare a leadership agenda that will serve to guide the church board in setting goals and assigning work groups.

"Does anyone have anything he or she would like to add to our agenda?"

During the prayer and sharing time, it is good to ask, "What is the item that caused you to say, 'Lord, I need special wisdom to deal with this issue in my church'? Did you have one that particularly concerned you?" At that point, if the pastor does not share a particular item from the survey, then the developer should cite one from his own experience. "You know, I remember a particular church that I was in, in which this problem seemed to be quite apparent" (name a problem). A personal example is effective. If not, you can follow a second tack in which you would say, "I have tried to think as if I were pastoring this church. If I were in Jim's shoes, which issue would I especially hold up before the Lord in prayer? I might choose this one." As you talk about the need for wisdom, you could say, "Are there any people that should be immediate members of your church, or people who are studying for baptism right now, that we need to remember in prayer?" Finally, remember the pastor's family, and by bringing it up, you alert the pastor and members to your priorities regarding a minister's home. This period of experiences, promises, and needs should conclude in prayer.

Perception Check

The developer should begin this session by asking the pastor for his list of strengths and weaknesses. Taking out his perception check worksheet, he will begin comparing his list with the pastor's. If the developer does not have his sheet filled out, he will communicate a lack of personal preparation, thereby forfeiting his leadership.

The perception check is vital in that it builds a rapport between the developer, the pastor and the lay leadership. The pastor must feel that he can reveal his and the church's needs. In order to arrive at this goal he must see that the developer understands their situation, thus building a confidence in the consultant's ability to be of real assistance. Therefore, it is important to:

1. Communicate acceptance of their priorities as opposed to insisting that they follow yours.

2. Gather information—ask for the reasons behind their evaluations. Draw them back to the profile for clarification. Explain your conclusions based on the profile. Utilize the data to support your conclusions.

3. Communicate an identity with the church's situation.

Leadership Agenda

The goal of this section is to aid the council in organizing the needs of the church in a manner that the board can utilize for goal setting. A copy of the leadership agenda worksheet follows.

Use the needs column to list the church's list of needs rated according to priority.

The assignment column will include which individuals,

church departments, or committees the church should ask to
develop strategies to meet the needs. This section should also
include a measurable suggested goal, such as: "To increase
family worship by 5 percent among our church families over
the next quarter." In some cases discuss the goal, but do not
place it on paper; this will allow the board the freedom of goal
setting without a suggestion. In either case a measurable goal
must be set by the board, the group, or by a negotiation
between the board and the group. Do not make nebulous
statements such as "to increase family worship" or "to
encourage Bible study." The first example is inappropriate
because it does not state a measurable number; the second
because it focuses on what the officers will do, not on what
they want to see happen among the people.

The resource section has three columns. In it the
developer and evangelism council brainstorm possible contri-
butions that the three groups could make in order to meet the
stated goal. This section also serves to lay the groundwork for
the pastor's personal assessment.

The *members'* column is the place to utilize the congregation's strength list. The council needs to examine the
congregation's own capacity to minister to itself. If this is done
in advance of the board meeting, the leaders will be able to
provide the necessary guidance the group will require in its
goal setting. These columns can remain blank when
submitted to the board. However, the pastor should fill them
out on his personal sheet during the consulting session.

The *pastor's* column will serve to explore strengths and
weaknesses.

The *conference* column is one that involves the developer.
He can inform the church of training events, funding
resources, and specific programs. And he can serve as an
invaluable aid to matching the public evangelists' approaches
to the needs of the church and community.

Church Board Planning Session

Present the results of the survey to the church board
members so that they can set specific goals for the spiritual life
of the congregation based on present reality. To prepare for

RESOURCES

Need	Assignment	Members	Pastor	Conference

the meeting, take the following steps:

1. Photocopy the church profile for each member.

2. Secure copies of the national profile so that you can compare your church with others in the North American Division.

3. Make sure that you have a blackboard or newsprint and chalk or markers.

The planning sessions that we conduct include the following agenda items:

1. Devotional—related to the spiritual life of the apostolic church (Acts 2:41, 42, or Eph. 3:15-21, et cetera).

2. Strengths and weaknesses—pass out the profiles and ask the board members to work in groups of two, evaluating the strengths and weaknesses in the manner described above.

3. Needs list—write on the board those discovered in the previous exercise.

4. Rank the needs in order of priority.

5. Assign them to groups to give study and recommend goals, resources, and strategies. Give special attention to assigning the needs to the departments that they relate to the most.

6. Explain additional profile options that can aid planning groups in targeting specific segments of the congregation. Example: If you find that your congregation needs to grow in the area of personal Bible study, you may introduce a seminar or retreat on the subject, only to find that it tends to attract those already studying the Bible regularly, thus missing for the most part the people you wanted to affect. You can avoid such problems by identifying the segment of your congregation that you wish to focus upon. To do this, you can request the Institute of Church Ministry to provide you with a profile of all the people who mark sometimes, never, or doesn't apply on the question regarding regular Bible study. The charge for this service is nominal, and the benefits to program planners are numerous.

7. Determine deadlines for reporting.

Exercises

1. Identify the strengths and weaknesses of Anytown

MAKING THE MOST OF A PROFILE

Church. Evaluate the responses to each question by placing a plus (+), a minus (−), or a question mark (?) beside the item. The meanings of the symbols are listed below:

    + = a strength
    − = a weakness
    ? = uncertain, not clear
  Example:

		None				Intimate
+ 3.	Circle the number that indicates your relation-ship with Christ.	1	2	3	4	5
		1	9	15	40	35

2. Jot down what you feel are the five most critical need areas of this church.

3. List what you feel are its strengths.

4. What do you feel would be an appropriate goal for this church to set in meeting need #1?

5. What strategy would you propose to meet this need?

10

Mobilizing the Members

Over a period of time the calling of pastor has evolved into a profession. At one time the minister might have been a layman who felt "called to preach." Then came short Bible courses, a Bachelor's degree in religion or theology, and finally, a full seminary training. Today, some pastors are even earning a Doctor of Ministry degree. "You've come a long way," pastor!

In many ways this is good. The general level of education in our society has skyrocketed, and the minister who would gain a hearing must keep up. But one major drawback has surfaced. As the minister has gained professional stature, the members have increasingly looked to him to do the work of the church—especially soul winning. Too many in the congregation—busy with their own pursuits—willingly turn church growth over to the pastor. After all, they reason, he is trained and paid to do it.

It wasn't always that way. In the early church, spreading the gospel was everybody's task. "All except the apostles were scattered throughout Judea and Samaria. . . . Those who had been scattered preached the word wherever they went" (Acts

8:1-4). No wonder that Christianity shook cities, and thousands joined the faith. Even today the active involvement of the laity is a principal reason for the phenomenal growth in Inter-America and South America.

Ellen White has told us that "the work of God in this earth can never be finished until the men and women comprising our church membership rally to the work, and unite their efforts with those of ministers and church officers."[1] No wonder that we're still here.

What the Research Shows

Do we have any evidence that the active participation of the laity can make a difference in church growth in North America? Consider some studies conducted by the Institute of Church Ministry.

ICM surveyed more than 7,800 members attending 112 churches in the Oregon Conference (nearly all the congregations in the conference) and the pastors of 107 of them.[2] Then we compared the survey questions with the actual and kingdom growth rates of those churches over a two-year period. The highest correlation of any question on the pastor survey with actual growth (.337) was "What percent of your membership is actively engaged in some form of personal outreach to nonmembers?" The second highest (.209 and .147 with kingdom growth) was "How effective have Bible studies by lay persons proved to be in this church for gaining baptisms?" Also, the question "Do you take lay members with you to Bible studies for training purposes?" showed significant relationship with both actual and kingdom growth, and the extent to which new converts were involved in church activity with kingdom growth.

On the member survey the highest correlation with actual (.300) and kingdom (.327) growth rates was the question "How many people have you been wholly or partially responsible for bringing into the church in the past three years?" We found this item also to be important in our surveys of Adventist members in the Washington, Texas, and Hawaiian conferences. Growing churches are likely to have more members who hold church offices or other service positions in Oregon, in Washington, and in the division-wide survey.

In Oregon the question "Have you engaged in some type of witnessing program over the past year?" had a significant relationship with actual growth (.189). "Have you held Bible studies with a non-Adventist this year?" correlated with actual (.233) and kingdom (.289) growth and was also important in the Washington study. Members involved in community outreach services such as Dorcas or the Five-Day Plan to Stop Smoking were more likely to be in growing churches in Oregon and Washington. And the Oregon, Washington, Hawaiian, and division-wide studies show a correspondence between growth and the extent that new members participate in church fellowship and activities.

Thus the empirical evidence supports the divine prescription. The pastor will not be able to finish the task by himself, no matter how talented he is or how hard he labors. It's going to take all of us. It's going to take a Caring Church.

How People Come Into the Church

It is only logical that churches will more likely grow if the pastor has some help and doesn't have to do all the work by himself. But are there additional reasons why a positive relationship exists between an active laity and church growth?

For one thing, consider the apostasy rate. Members actively sharing their faith and leading others to the Lord are not nearly as likely to become discouraged and drop out. But research has revealed that unless the congregation gives a person a role in the church, a task to perform, or a group to join, within one year he or she will likely become inactive. And apostasy has a powerful influence in retarding church growth.

An even more important reason lies in the way people enter the church. For most individuals the initial contact that may eventually lead to church membership comes through a relative or close friend.

The New Testament seems to anticipate this. In Acts 16 the conversion of Lydia resulted in the baptism of the members of her household (verse 15), and the jailer of the prison that held Paul and Silas was baptized with all his family (verse 33). Cornelius had called together his relatives and close friends to hear the gospel message from Peter (chap. 10:24), and Jesus told the man He had freed from demon possession to "'go home to your family and tell them how much the Lord has done for you, and how he has had mercy on you'" (Mark 5:19). Here is the most natural, fruitful, and cost-effective way to make churches grow.

Win Arn has asked more than fourteen thousand Christians of many denominations and in a variety of settings about that first contact with the church that finally led them down the road to membership. The results of this poll are most instructive.[3] Those who simply walked into the church constitute about 3 to 4 percent; those attracted by the church program, 2 to 3 percent; those found by the pastor, 2 to 3 percent; those who had some special need in their lives that led them to seek the church, 2 to 4 percent; those found in an intensive visitation program, 1 to 2 percent; those brought in through the Sunday school, 3 to 4 percent; those coming to an evangelistic crusade or watching a TV program, less than 1 percent; but those whose first contact was with a friend or relative totaled between 70 and 90 percent.

With Adventists the percentage whose first contact involved an evangelistic series would probably be higher. Some have suggested as much as 5 to 10 percent. A two-year survey of new converts in the Georgia-Cumberland Conference produced a figure of 8.5 percent. But most converts baptized in a crusade did not simply respond to the advertising. A friend or relative brought them to the meetings. We are not suggesting that the other means have no importance in making Adventists. It is to say that they usually do not get the chance to play their part unless someone who can gain the hearing of the prospect because of the close relationship between them has first opened the door.

Therefore, as a part of its growth strategy, the church will carefully study the networks or "webs" surrounding the present membership. They will consist of immediate family, close friends, relatives, job associates, neighbors, and more casual acquaintances. Win Arn claims that the average member can list between eight and nine people within the sphere of his/her influence who are within reasonable driving distance. These names represent some of the finest prospects for church growth.

Not only that, but the network expands every time a new member joins the church. For each new member has some close friends and relatives within his/her circle of influence not yet already included in the webs of other members. Actually, the new convert usually has far greater evangelistic potential than the longtme member. He/she will more likely have a web of close acquaintances who are not already members of the congregation.

Motivating the Members

Obviously, the mobilization of the laity is one of the essentials of church growth. But how do you get them to do it? Most pastors know that they need the members, but often feel that the task of getting them involved is akin to waking up the dead.

Some traditional approaches we cannot recommend because they usually have the opposite of the desired effect. One is to peddle guilt. "You're not a real Christian if you don't get out and witness." "Nobody is going to be in heaven who hasn't brought someone with him." "If you don't evangelize, you will fossilize." Such rantings rarely accomplish more than to cause the congregation to feel so uncomfortable that they wish to replace the pastor with one who will speak more positively. Negatives simply do not motivate people.

Some stress the sense of duty. "The church is counting on you." "You should do this to show your love for the Lord." The response often is, "I know I should, but I can't." So more guilt.

Finally, we have the promise of eternal reward. "It will be a star in your crown." "You will be saving yourself while you are saving others." Basically this motive appeals to selfish interests. Not only that, but it puts the satisfactions so far in the future that they seem small in comparison to the present hurdles to overcome.

So what approach should we use? One of the most important is to get the congregation to "own" the goals by involving them in every phase of the goal setting and strategy planning as described in the chapters on "Owning Goals" and "A Model for Church Planning."

Some other thoughts that may prove helpful we have gleaned from the book by McGavran and Hunter[4] and from lectures by Douglas Johnson,[5] Carl George,[6] and Monte Sahlin.[7]

A powerful urge dwells in the bosom of every human being to want to please his/her parents unless a long history of negative experiences has built up an insurmountable wall between them. So we have an inborn longing to please the heavenly Father. Everyone who has heard the gospel wants to obey God's call and is more disappointed with his/her own failures than the preacher ever could be in his most scolding moment. Motivation is not whipping people up into action. It is channeling their own desires into bridges that lead to success.

Sahlin lists some of the essential elements in a program for motivating volunteers:

1. A sense of community (the opportunity for friendships).

2. A chance for personal growth and development.

3. Participation by volunteers in problem solving and significant decision making.

4. Choices of programs related to individual interests and needs.

5. An explicit contract regarding time and level of commitment.

6. Opportunities for study and joint planning of goals.

7. Regular mechanisms for supportive feedback.

8. Meaningful orientation and training activities.

One reason, then, why members may not enlist in the task of the church is because they are mismatched with the job. The first principle of good administration is to have your objectives clearly in sight. The second is to have the right person doing the right job to reach those objectives. We may have the right person doing the wrong job. Or the wrong person doing the right job. Or perhaps we have yet to identify the right job.

A second reason for the low volunteer rate is that busywork may have bored the members. They have plenty to do, but the jobs offered don't really make a difference. Sometimes the tasks are vestiges from earlier stages of development and not related to present overall goals and mission. A third reason may be that the members do not know how to work for the Lord. They lack a concept of their roles or don't have the skills and training needed to perform them.

All of this suggests that we must help church members to find ways by which they can meet their deep inner needs to please God and to find personal significance. Today, more than at any time in the past, volunteers search for personal meaning. They gain satisfaction and joy from helping others and from knowing that their efforts make a difference. But they must obtain a payoff or they won't stay on the job long. God brings a sense of divine approval to those performing within the area of their spiritual gifts. Helping a person to receive satisfaction from a task is a good clue to knowing what God wants him or her to do.

The dynamics of the volunteer worker also make it imperative that the church provide social support for those involved in evangelistic ministry. When active lay members do not receive it, burnout will likely take place. Occasions like potlucks, outings, and joint recreation build morale and create esprit de corps. Often the spiritual health of the leader determines the health of the group. Each department needs a leader who can model the spiritual tone. Others will find wholeness and purpose in the presence of such an individual.

The efforts of "behind-the-line" or "backup" workers are also vital to social support. Not everybody in the church serves on the front line, but all can have a sense of mission, since they may sustain and make possible the work of the front-line troops. Church leaders must give them strokes and recognition for their efforts.

In the frantic economy of the late twentieth century, people are busier than ever before and by and large will have less time for church activities. More women (the former core of the volunteer force) work outside the home, and more men moonlight. The church can take this into account by asking them to perform specific tasks with terminal dates rather than calling for long-term or open-ended commitments. Organizations must plan for people to come in, stay awhile, and drop out. Some suggest that it is a good plan to change one third of the leadership each year, so we will always have a mix of the new and the inexperienced. It allows members to change jobs now and then or to rest out a year.

In order to accommodate volunteers, the local church may have to make several changes in its structure: (1) The congregation that wishes to mobilize its laity must free its pastor to recruit, train, and evaluate volunteers—probably his most important task; (2) lay members will have to take a more active part in recruiting and training others; (3) the schedule of volunteers must develop around their available time, rather than the convenience of the church.

The church must have a way to keep score and provide feedback if a lay mobilization is to succeed. If nobody pays attention to what happens, volunteers tend to think the job doesn't really matter, lose their sense of mission, and eventually quit trying. It is well to have graphs and other goal devices in which *one person* makes a difference in charting progress toward the goal (never use them to shame or embarrass members into participating, however). It is a law of human behavior that what you pay attention to will happen. The span of control in supervision should be small enough so that every worker receives a sincere compliment every week.

Finally, we must resist the temptation to try to force every person into the same mold. People can serve the church in many different ways. Everybody does *not* have to go door to door handing out printed material or attempting to secure Bible studies in order to be an active Christian. The Holy Spirit has distributed various spiritual gifts, all necessary for building up the body of the church. We best motivate and mobilize our memberships when we help them to discover, develop, and utilize the particular ones with which God has endowed them.

Working With the Power Structure [8]

When we talk about mobilizing all of the membership that

each might exercise his/her specific gift to make possible new feats in church growth, we anticipate some resistance from the power structure. Some longtime local leaders—official or unofficial—are used to seeing things done in a certain way and may resent any change. They may be uncomfortable with a surge of activity from the younger group, with new and expensive projects, or with alternative standards of living and worship.

It is important to understand the thinking of the present leaders. The church has been called an *institution* of *change.* The two terms suggest opposing positions. While the church must constantly work to bring about renewal, it must also preserve basic values of the past. Therefore, it exists in a creative tension. The pastor who would lead his church in fulfilling its mission will heed well the warning Do not defy the power structure.

Rather, note that the present leadership is probably overburdened, and it would be difficult to extend the activities of the congregation by using their services. So appreciate and maintain the power structure in their present jobs, but find new people to extend current activities into additional areas or to start new ones.

Identify the five most powerful people and the five most powerful organizations that you have to work with within the church. Affirm them. Use their language. Talk so they can respond. Preserve and support the basic values. Determine the extent to which you can urge change without reaching the point where vitality drops and rebellion begins.

Above all, don't waste time and energy trying to push through insignificant alterations (such as bulletin formats and order of worship service). Use change where it really counts—to affect the mission and ministry of the church.

And always remember: "The work of God in this earth can never be finished until the men and women comprising our church membership rally to the work, and unite their efforts with those of ministers and church officers." [9]

Exercise

Identify your personal web of influence.

First, list all members of your immediate and extended family who are not members. Then make a judgment as to the receptivity of each (cold, uninterested to warm, interested) and suggest a strategy for cultivating his/her interest. Then move out in increasing circles of influence.

Relationship   *Name*   *Receptivity*   *Strategy*
Family
Friends
Work associates
Neighbors
Business contacts

References

[1] Ellen G. White, *Gospel Workers*, p. 352.
[2] Roger L. Dudley, Des Cummings, Jr., and Don Ritterskamp, "A Study of Factors Related to Church Growth in the Oregon Conference of Seventh-day Adventists" (Berrien Springs, Mich.: Institute of Church Ministry, 1982).
[3] Lecture at the seminar on church growth held at Andrews University, September 2, 1982.
[4] McGavran and Hunter, *Church Growth: Strategies That Work*, pp. 46-52.
[5] Lecture at seminar on church growth, Sept. 1, 1982.
[6] Lecture at seminar on church growth, Aug. 29, 1982.
[7] Lecture at seminar on church growth, Aug. 30, 1982.
[8] From "The Caring Church" seminar held at Andrews University, March 21-23, 1982.
[9] White, *loc. cit.*

11

Whom Are We Winning?

Conducting any program without a proper evaluation is like shooting in the dark, hoping to hit something. The same applies to church growth. After all the praying and planning and programming, the church must attempt to discover how successful its efforts have been. A number of ways exist to do this. One is to examine the characteristics of the new converts.

Counting the number of persons added to the church over a given period is, of course, one measure of success. But it is a rather rough evaluation for it doesn't reveal either the target populations appealed to most effectively or the methods that produce the greatest results. We must have a more discriminating gauge.

To meet this need the Institute of Church Ministry has developed the New Member Survey. We designed it to use with converts who have been in the church less than a year. Several conferences are employing it to gather information from all newly baptized members. A copy of it appears here.

ICM developed the instrument so you could use it in conjunction with the demographic profile of your church territory. When employed in this manner, it will provide the

New Member Survey

1. Before you became a Seventh-day Adventist, what was your religious background? Circle the number.

   1. No church membership
   2. Raised in an Adventist home
   3. Protestant (please specify denomination)_____
   4. Catholic
   5. Other religion_____

2. Which factor most attracted you to the Adventist church? Circle the number.

   1. Raised an Adventist and simply accepted parental values
   2. Truth and beauty of the church's teachings
   3. Warm fellowship among the members
   4. Charisma of the minister/evangelist
   5. Personal contact with a church member
   6. Adventist radio or television program

3. Did any of the following events disrupt your regular life pattern during the 12 months just before you became an Adventist? Circle 1 for yes and 2 for no.

YES	NO	
1	2	Personal illness or injury
1	2	Death or serious illness of a close friend or relative
1	2	Marriage
1	2	Divorce or marital problems
1	2	Birth or adoption of a child
1	2	Son or daughter leaving home
1	2	Retirement
1	2	Loss of job
1	2	Change to a different line of work
1	2	Moved to another area
1	2	Severe financial difficulties
1	2	Legal problems
1	2	Other personal or family emotional crisis

4. Please indicate how much of an influence each source listed below was toward your joining the Adventist church. Circle the appropriate number.

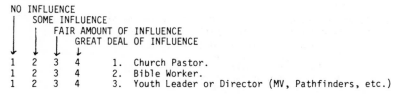

NO INFLUENCE
  SOME INFLUENCE
    FAIR AMOUNT OF INFLUENCE
      GREAT DEAL OF INFLUENCE

   1 2 3 4   1. Church Pastor.
   1 2 3 4   2. Bible Worker.
   1 2 3 4   3. Youth Leader or Director (MV, Pathfinders, etc.)

```
NO INFLUENCE
 |    SOME INFLUENCE
 |     |   FAIR AMOUNT OF INFLUENCE
 |     |    |   GREAT DEAL OF INFLUENCE
 ↓     ↓    ↓    ↓
 1     2    3    4      4.  Adventist Book Salesman.
 1     2    3    4      5.  Medical or health personnel not in an Adventist
                            hospital.
 1     2    3    4      6.  Medical or health personnel in an Adventist
                            hospital.
 1     2    3    4      7.  An Adventist member whom you did not know,
                            witnessing door-to-door.
 1     2    3    4      8.  Relative.
 1     2    3    4      9.  Adventist neighbor.
 1     2    3    4     10.  Work, business or professional acquaintance.
 1     2    3    4     11.  Other Adventist acquaintance (Please specify
                            type of acquaintance.)
 1     2    3    4     12.  Seventh-day Adventist Community Service Center.
 1     2    3    4     13.  Bible Correspondence Lessons.
 1     2    3    4     14.  Bible Lessons with a church member in your home.
 1     2    3    4     15.  Bible classes in the church.
 1     2    3    4     16.  Series of public meetings (such as evangelistic
                            meetings in the church.)
 1     2    3    4     17.  Ingathering.
 1     2    3    4     18.  Adventist school, academy, college, university.
 1     2    3    4     19.  Voice of Prophecy radio program.
 1     2    3    4     20.  It Is Written television program.
 1     2    3    4     21.  Faith for Today television program.
 1     2    3    4     22.  Breath of Life television program.
 1     2    3    4     23.  La Voz de la Esperanza radio program.
 1     2    3    4     24.  Amazing Facts.
 1     2    3    4     25.  Vacation Bible School.
 1     2    3    4     26.  Junior or Youth Camp.
 1     2    3    4     27.  Seventh-day Adventist books, magazines or
                            other publications.
 1     2    3    4     28.  Health program or classes, such as: Five-Day
                            Plan to Stop Smoking, Cooking School, etc.
```

5. Please enter the number of the ONE source from the list in question #4
   through which you FIRST became attracted to the Adventist church.

   #_____

6. If you attended evangelistic meetings prior to becoming an Adventist,
   how did you learn of them? Circle the number.

        1. Advertising in the mail or at your door
        2. Newspaper advertising
        3. Radio or TV advertising
        4. Invitation by family member
        5. Invitation by friend
        6. Invitation by speaker or team member
        7. Invitation by church member whom you didn't know

7. How many years did you attend Seventh-day Adventist schools on each
   of the following levels? Count a part of a year as a full year.
   a. Elementary (grades 1-8) _____
   b. Academy (grades 9-12) _____
   c. College/university _____

8. How helpful do you find the following resources in strengthening your
   spiritual life and Christian experience. Circle the appropriate number.

   NOT HELPFUL
   | SOMEWHAT HELPFUL
   | | VERY HELPFUL
   ↓ ↓ ↓
   1 2 3   Sabbath School
   1 2 3   Church service
   1 2 3   Prayer meeting
   1 2 3   Personal Bible study
   1 2 3   Ellen White writings
   1 2 3   The Adventist Review
   1 2 3   Other magazines
   1 2 3   Adventist radio and television programs

9. Since becoming an Adventist, have you used the following methods of
   witnessing for Christ? Circle 1 for yes and 2 for no.

   YES NO
   1   2   Giving Bible studies
   1   2   Inviting a non-Adventist to public meetings or to church
   1   2   Giving out literature
   1   2   Sharing your personal testimony of what God has done
           for you
   1   2   Working in community services
   1   2   Teaching a Sabbath School class
   1   2   Giving out Adventist radio/TV logs
   1   2   Following up media interests with personal calls

10. Which statement below comes the nearest to describing the type of
    fellowship you have found in the Adventist church? Circle the
    number.

    1. Cold and exclusive. I don't feel at home.
    2. People are friendly, but I haven't developed any close
       relationships.
    3. A friendly atmosphere. I've made some good friends.
    4. Very warm and loving. Like a family.

11. How do you rate your present relationship to the church? Circle a
    number.

    1. Very weak. Just hanging on.
    2. Somewhat lukewarm.
    3. Average.
    4. Strong. Participate regularly in most activities.
    5. Very active. On fire for God.

12. Your age _____ years

13. Your sex
    1. male
    2. female

14. Your marital status
    1. single
    2. married
    3. divorced
    4. separated
    5. widowed

15. Your ethnic background
    1. Asian
    2. Black
    3. Hispanic
    4. Oriental
    5. White
    6. Other

16. Your yearly family income
    1. Under $6,000
    2. 6,000 - 9,999
    3. 10,000 - 14,999
    4. 15,000 - 24,999
    5. 25,000 - 50,000
    6. over $50,000

17. What is the highest level of formal education that you have completed?

    _____

18. What is your occupation?

    _____

19. Please use the space below to tell in a few words what about the
    Adventist church means the most to you.

THANK YOU

church-growth planning team with the information necessary to identify groups that would be most "winnable." How is this possible?

1. The New Member Survey helps you to identify the type of people your church/conference or evangelists have been reaching.

2. The demographic information helps you identify the location of these categories within your territory.

3. You can then target these populations with direct mail, advertising, Bible study cards, et cetera, in order to maximize the effectiveness of current programs. It represents a great improvement of stewardship in that instead of mass mailing fifty thousand handbills throughout the city, you can buy the mailing list containing individuals most receptive to the particular method of public evangelism.

4. Demographics will assist you in determining the kinds of people in your community your present techniques of evangelism are not touching. This will allow you to research them to discover their felt needs and experiment with new approaches of evangelism. In order to assure future evangelistic effectiveness, this is especially critical.

The New Member Survey can help match an evangelist's skills to the needs of a community. For example, if an evangelist asks each individual he baptizes to assist him by filling out a New Member Survey, in a short time he will be able to determine which populations he most effectively reaches. This is beneficial in two ways: first, advertising agencies can assist you much more when they know which population you are trying to contact, and second, you can identify cities that should especially respond to your style of evangelism.

You will notice that the survey starts with the religious background of the convert and then probes the kinds of influences, both as to time and to strength, that led him/her into the church. Several questions then explore the new member's experience within the church in areas such as spiritual resources, witnessing, fellowship, and perseverance. The survey concludes by gathering some valuable demographic information.

A Sample Profile

The Institute of Church Ministry has also developed a computer profile to display the results of a particular survey in a manner that will make them easily readable. The profile could depict converts brought into a particular church, those becoming members during a particular evangelistic campaign even though they might join several local congregations, those converted in a specific area of the conference, or the new additions to an entire conference. We have provided a sample profile here as an illustration.

It represents eighty-six people baptized by a city evangelist in a major metropolitan area of the United States. Since the New Member Survey displayed is a newly revised edition, the profile, based on the first edition of the survey, differs slightly from the survey shown here.

Question 1 reveals that only 8 percent of the converts had an Adventist background, quite different from the usual profile, which reveals a heavy baptism of congregational children and former members. The bulk of the converts divide equally between Protestants and Catholics. An inspection of the supplementary table shows that of the 42 percent who are Protestants, more than half came from Lutheran or Baptist churches.

Question 2 indicates that the Adventist message must have come through "loud and clear" in this campaign, since a large majority (79 percent) found the truth and beauty of the church's teachings to be the most persuasive factor in their decision to join the church, and only 3 percent felt that the personality of the minister had primarily swayed them.

While most people, according to question 3, did not experience a disruption of their life pattern just prior to their conversions, 17 percent had moved from another area, and 28 percent had had some personal or family emotional crisis. This may indicate more fruitful target populations.

Combining "fair amount of influence" and "great deal of influence" on question 4 provides opportunity to measure the relative strength of the various evangelistic methods *in this situation*. Since these are converts from a series of meetings, it

NEW MEMBER SURVEY
Institute of Church Ministry
Theological Seminary, Andrews University

Number of surveys for this report = 86

1. Before you became a Seventh-day Adventist, what was your religious background?

No membership	Raised SDA	Protestant	Catholic	Other
8%	8%	42%	42%	40%

For further breakdown see accompanying table.

2. Which factor most attracted you to the Adventist church?

Raised SDA	Church's teachings	Member fellowship	Minister charisma	Other
1%	79%	9%	3%	1%

3. Did any of the following events disrupt your regular life pattern during the 12 months just before you became an Adventist?

	Yes	No
Personal illness or injury	12%	88%
Death or serious illness of a close friend or relative	14%	86%
Marriage	9%	91%
Divorce or marital problems	14%	86%
Birth or adoption of a child	2%	98%
Son or daughter leaving home	5%	95%
Retirement	0%	100%
Loss of job	10%	90%
Change to a different line of work	9%	91%
Moved to another area	17%	83%
Severe financial difficulties	15%	85%
Legal problems	2%	98%
Other personal or family emotional crisis	28%	72%

4. Please indicate how much of an influence each source listed below was toward your joining the Adventist church.
N—No influence
S—Some influence
F—Fair amount of influence
G—Great deal of influence

	N	S	F	G
1. Church pastor	14%	13%	13%	60%
2. Bible worker	28%	15%	16%	41%
3. Youth leader or director	?	?	?	?
4. Adventist book salesman	99%	1%	0%	0%
5. Medical or health personnel not in SDA hospital	91%	6%	3%	0%
6. Medical or health personnel in SDA hospital	92%	6%	0%	2%
7. An SDA member whom you did not know, witnessing door to door	88%	3%	1%	7%
8. Relative	74%	1%	5%	20%
9. Adventist neighbor	92%	3%	0%	5%
10. Work, business or professional acquaintance	95%	2%	0%	2%
11. Other Adventist acquaintance	71%	6%	5%	19%
12. SDA Community Service Center	98%	2%	0%	0%
13. Bible correspondence lessons	85%	2%	5%	3%
14. Bible lessons with a church member in your home	44%	7%	9%	40%
15. Bible classes in the church	40%	12%	21%	28%
16. Series of public meetings	13%	3%	13%	71%
17. Musical group				
18. SDA school, academy, college, university	84%	12%	3%	1%
19. SDA radio, TV program				

24. Health program or classes

25. Other sources

5. For results to this question see supplementary table.

6. If you attended evangelistic meetings prior to becoming an Adventist, how did you learn of them?

Mail/door	Newspaper	Radio/TV ad.	Family invitation	Friend invitation	Member invitation	Speaker invitation	Other
48%	3%	4%	8%	24%	4%	3%	7%

7. How many years did you attend Seventh-day Adventist schools on each of the following levels? Count a part of a year as a full year.

	1	2	3	4	5	6	7	8	None
A) Elementary	0%	2%	1%	3%	0%	0%	0%	0%	93%
B) Academy	1%	2%	0%	2%		0%			99%
C) College	1%					0%			99%

8. How helpful do you find the following resources in strengthening your spiritual life and Christian experience?

	Not helpful	Some help	Very helpful
Sabbath school	3%	16%	80%
Church service	0%	8%	92%
Prayer meeting	29%	19%	52%
Personal Bible study	9%	15%	76%
Ellen White writings	12%	22%	66%
Adventist Review	36%	50%	14%
Other magazines	32%	29%	39%

9. Since becoming an Adventist, have you used the following methods of witnessing for Christ?

	Yes	No
A) Giving Bible studies	43%	57%
B) Inviting people to church or evangelistic meetings	86%	14%
C) Giving out literature	88%	12%
D) Sharing personal testimony	86%	14%
E) Working in community services	28%	72%
F) Teaching a Sabbath School class	20%	80%
G) Other means	22%	78%

10. Which statement below comes the nearest to describing the type of fellowship you have found in the Adventist church?

Cold and exclusive	Friendly but not close	Friendly atmosphere	Warm and loving
0%	12%	36%	52%

11. How do you rate your present relationship to the church?

Very weak	Lukewarm	Average	Strong	On fire
3%	3%	33%	42%	19%

12. Your age

19 years or under	20-35 years	36-50 years	51-65 years	Over 65 years
6%	46%	26%	19%	45%

13. Your sex

Male	Female
35%	65%

14. Your marital status

Single	Married	Divorced	Separated	Widowed	Other
29%	63%	6%	1%	15%	??%

15. Your ethnic background

White	Hispanic	Black	Oriental	Native American	Other
??%	??%	??%	??%	??%	??%

16. Your yearly family income

Under $6,000	$6,000-$9,999	$10,000-$14,999	$15,000-$24,999	$25,000-$50,000	Above $50,000
9%	10%	12%	32%	35%	2%

17. The type of community you lived in when you became an Adventist.

Rural	Small town	Medium town	Large city	Suburb over 100,000	Inner city over 100,000
1%	6%	25%	12%	45%	12%

18. What is the highest level of formal education that you have completed?

Less elem. grad.	Elem. grad.	Some high school	High school grad.	Some college	College grad.	Post-grad.
1%	5%	11%	33%	34%	13%	4%

19. What is your occupation?

Profes./Manag.	Government	Sale	Clerical	Skilled Labor	Unskilled Labor	Homemaker	Student	Retired
30%	1%	6%	16%	12%	4%	23%	4%	4%

20. Your political affiliation

Democrat	Republican	Independent
24%	28%	47%

NEW MEMBER SURVEY
Supplementary Tables

Question 1, response 3, Protestant background—42%

Denomination	Percentage of Total
No response	1%
Baptist	8%
Presbyterian	4%
Episcopal	1%
Methodist	6%
Lutheran	14%
Pentecostal	2%
Church of Christ	5%
United Brethren	1%
	42%

Question 5: Number of source in question 4 which was *first* contact with Adventist church.

Number	Percentage of Total
0	2%
2	2%
4	4%
6	2%
7	2%
8	21%
9	2%
10	4%
11	5%
14	4%
16	36%
17	1%
19	7%
24	3%
25	5%

is not surprising that they rated this method highest (84 percent). (The results are usually far different when we consider all converts in a given church or conference.) The pastor (73 percent) and the Bible worker (57 percent) also do well. Forty-nine percent regarded Bible lessons in the home and Bible classes in the church as a high factor, and 33 percent felt themselves rather strongly influenced by our publications. The supplementary table on question 5 reveals that for 36 percent the first contact with the church was the meetings themselves, while 21 percent initially encountered Adventism through a relative.

By far the largest number (48 percent) learned of the meetings through an advertisement received in the mail or delivered at their door. Another 24 percent had a friend invite them. Newspaper or radio/TV ads did not pull well in this situation.

According to question 9 a large majority of the new converts actively witness by inviting friends to meetings, giving out literature, and sharing their personal experiences. A significant minority even conduct Bible studies.

Most of the new members have found their churches to be friendly or warm and loving, but a small group (12 percent) are having difficulty in forming close friendships. Three fourths of the converts rate their present relationship to the church as either average or strong, and 19 percent feel on fire for God.

On the demographic questions, 72 percent are between 20 and 50 years of age. They will be a strength to the church, since these are key leadership years. On the other hand, one notices an unusually heavy tilt toward female converts. Why not more men? The converts are mostly white—especially since, given the area, one suspects that the 8 percent "native Americans" are Caucasians who have misunderstood the question.

The group is quite well educated, with 84 percent having at least a high school diploma and more than half having some college. We find this reflected in the occupations, where the largest group is in professional or managerial positions, and only 4 percent classify themselves as unskilled laborers.

ADVENTURES IN CHURCH GROWTH

The Lake Union Soul-Winning Institute in Chicago has successfully employed this approach combined with demographic studies. Their work has demonstrated how the use of research tools can dramatically increase results in evangelism for the same number of dollars spent and enable Adventists to be more effective and to get more for their money.

LUSI has employed these methods to identify target population groups and plant new churches. Recently the Institute of Church Ministry at Andrews University did a computerized study on the city of Chicago to help identify population groups that would be open and receptive to planting new Adventist congregations. One such area that the survey uncovered was the old Midway Airport area in Chicago, known as the Marquette Park/Garfield Ridge area. Surprisingly enough, the area had 180,000 people living within it, approximately 70,000 households, and no Seventh-day Adventist church. It is a lower-middle-class, basically white population, with incomes ranging from $18,000 to $21,000. LUSI has now established an Adventist congregation there.

The Institute has also used the New Member Survey to determine the kind of people they are reaching in Chicago. The facts uncovered have enabled them to analyze their approaches in advertising and have helped them to broaden out to those segments of the population that they do not yet touch. Also, the results enable them to strengthen their approach for those that they are influencing. It's an exciting thing to recognize that the Holy Spirit can enable evangelists to be more effective by increasing the tools that they have at their command.

A Conference-wide Study

It is easy to see how such a profile could provide valuable information for a local congregation or a particular evangelist in evaluating the results of a church growth thrust. But what about a wider area? How could a conference employ it to determine the effectiveness of its various evangelistic strategies? The Institute of Church Ministry conducted such a study for the Georgia-Cumberland Conference, surveying a sampling of new converts over a two-year period. Here are some of the highlights:

The Georgia-Cumberland New Member Study surveyed 339 of the total 1,554 new members (22 percent) baptized into the Georgia-Cumberland Conference from January 1, 1979, through December 31, 1980. The project sought to discover which approaches yielded the greatest success and to specify the demographics of the most winnable populations. The results were divided into three sections: (1) a descriptive profile of the total group of new members, (2) a descriptive comparison of the new members with no Adventist religious background, and (3) a comparison of the weak, average, and strong new members (question 11).

Summary of Section One. The prominent results of the descriptive profile on the total group of new members from the Georgia-Cumberland Conference revealed that they came from either a Protestant (45 percent) or Seventh-day Adventist (38 percent) religious background. The majority (51 percent) considered themselves attracted to the Adventist Church because of the truth and beauty of its teachings. The new members first became acquainted with the church through a relative (36 percent) or church pastor (11 percent), and the pastor (49 percent), relative (37 percent), and public meetings (33 percent) had the strongest influences in their joining. If they attended evangelistic meetings, they learned of them by family members (39 percent), advertising in the mail or at the door (33 percent), or invitation by friends (22 percent).

A majority of the new members had participated in witnessing activities by giving out printed material (67 percent), inviting non-Adventists to meetings (66 percent), and sharing their personal testimony (60 percent). Nearly 85 percent said they found at least a friendly atmosphere and some good friends in the church, and more than 45 percent said they were strong in their relationship to the church.

Demographic information showed that the average age was about 28 years, with 73 percent 36 or under. The male-to-female ratio was about 46 to 54. About 45 percent were married and 45 percent single. The educational level of the new members averaged tenth grade, with 45 percent completing high school and 8 percent college. Only 36 percent indicated attendance at Adventist elementary schools, 7 percent at academies, and 4 percent at Adventist colleges. The majority (85 percent) were white and English-speaking, with the remainder divided among native American, Oriental, black, and Hispanic. The yearly family income spread evenly over the income brackets, except that only 2 percent earned more than $50,000. The occupations were primarily students (38 percent), professional/managerial (14 percent), and homemakers (14 percent). The new members displayed fairly even distribution over the political affiliations (Independent, Democrat, and Republican).

Summary of Section Two. The results of the descriptive comparison of the new members with no Adventist background revealed some differences. One would expect those questions involving age, educational level, marital status, and occupations to change because of the younger age of the new members with Adventist background (biological growth). Other areas in which we observed significant differences included a drop in the influence of relatives and Seventh-day Adventist schools in bringing the new members into the church, an increase in the importance of the truth and beauty of the church's teachings as an attracting factor, an increase in witnessing activities involving more personal contact, a higher percentage of females than males, a slight increase in the percentage of new members in the lower income brackets, and a slightly higher chance of having some disruptive event in their lives.

Questions showing little change included the source of first acquaintance with the church, resources in strengthening spiritual life and Christian experience, type of fellowship found in the church, present relationship to the church, ethnic background, type of community lived in before joining the church, and political affiliation.

Summary of Section Three. The results of the comparison of the weak, average, and strong new members from the Georgia-Cumberland Conference revealed that a greater percentage of new members with an Adventist religious background tended to rate themselves as stronger members, while the new members with no church membership or Protestant religious background tended to classify themselves as weaker. Those new members who united with the church because of the truth and beauty of its teachings tended to regard themselves as stronger than those who joined because of the charisma of the minister/evangelist. New members who indicated a recent death or illness of a close friend or relative had a greater percentage in the strong profile, while those who acknowledged a recent birth or adoption of a child, severe financial difficulties, or other personal or family emotional crises had a greater percentage in the weak category. Individuals who felt they had strong ties with the church considered the writings of Ellen White and magazines as more helpful to their spiritual life than those with a weak relationship. The new members in the strong profile tended to be more involved in witnessing activities (except Bible studies) than those in the weak one. The stronger new members tended to find the church warmer and friendlier than the weaker ones.

Concerning demographic information, the new members 19 and under and those 51 and over contained a higher percentage in the strong category than in the weak, but had the greatest percentage in the average category. The 20-to-35 and 36-to-50 age groups displayed a higher percentage in the weak profile. Those new members indicating some attendance at Adventist elementary schools had a greater percentage in the strong category, while those who had never gone to Adventist elementary schools had a greater percentage in the weak category.

The single new converts tended to rate themselves as stronger members, while the divorced tended to classify themselves as weaker. The higher the income level, the more likely the new members rated themselves as strong. Additions from the small and medium-sized towns generally saw themselves stronger, while those from rural communities, large cities, suburbs, or inner cities fell into the weaker category. The homemakers usually rated themselves as weaker in their relationship to the church, while the students ranked themselves as stronger. Converts indicating a Democratic political affiliation regarded themselves as weaker, while those with a Republican or Independent affiliation for the most part viewed themselves as stronger.

Two elements become most important as we analyze these results. First, we clearly see the importance of the influence of some member of the Adventist community (pastor, relative, church member, Adventist acquaintance, Bible worker). Second, there appears to be a strong emphasis on the Biblical study of Adventist teachings (public meetings, Bible classes in the church, Bible lessons with a church member, Bible correspondence lessons). Thus the evangelistic methods yielding the greatest success are those involving a Biblical study of Adventist teachings with a personal contact with some member of the Adventist community.

The survey findings, along with a demographic profile of the Atlanta area, helped identify the most receptive groups in Greater Atlanta. The conference and ICM zeroed in on twenty-three census tracts as prime areas for Adventist Church growth. Conference officials, pastors, and church members have united to target them.

The Southern California, Northern California, and Ohio conferences have utilized this procedure in order to maximize evangelistic impact. We believe that church growth planners need this type of information for effective planning.

The two studies described in this chapter yield findings that are quite different from each other. Every church, conference, or other area has its own unique profile of new members. Only as we carefully study them is it possible to determine just whom we are reaching and on which groups we have little or no influence. The study also allows us to see which methods most effectively touch what target populations in our area. Finally, we can chart the progress of integrating the new members into the life and service of the congregation.

12

The Ogre of Apostasy

" 'Because of the increase of wickedness, the love of most will grow cold, but he who stands firm to the end will be saved' " (Matt. 24:12, 13).

Of all the ugly words in the Adventist vocabulary, the most horrible is surely "apostasy." It brings a cold chill and connotes a hopeless dread. Scattered throughout North America are scores of thousands—perhaps hundreds of thousands—of ex-Seventh-day Adventists. In some communities their numbers may approach that of the active membership. They appear in all walks of life, including government, show business, and prison. Their presence is the plague spot on the Adventist mission.

If significant church growth is to take place, we must find more effective methods—both preventive and remedial—of dealing with this problem. Controlling apostasy is absolutely essential to the mission of the church. A member who does not apostatize contributes as much to growth as a new convert. If the number of apostasies equals the number of baptisms, no growth will take place even though large numbers may join. All of our research reveals that dealing with apostasy is an important component of any successful church growth program.

However, before looking at the results of some correlational studies, we must point out that apostasy as a variable is difficult to interpret. The steps a person takes that lead him to reject his relationship with Christ and the church are usually gradual and occur over an extended period of time. A gap exists between the time that a member turns away from the church in heart and the point where the congregation actually drops his/her name. Therefore, we must observe caution in relating apostasy to other attitudes and behaviors, since the real variable may be *dealing* with apostasy, rather than the actual disaffiliating process. Nevertheless, the research results are instructive.

Correlates of Apostasy

In our division-wide study of church growth[1] we found that the average number of apostasies in the 249 churches studied for the period of January 1, 1979 to June 30, 1980, was 5.6, or 3.73 per year. Their number tends to increase with the size of the church, which is logical, since there are more possibilities for dropouts. The number of apostasies also has a relationship, though a somewhat weak one, to the number of baptisms. It may mean that congregations are more willing to drop names when they are also adding some new ones through fresh conversions. However, more likely we can explain the relationship by the fact that both apostasy and baptism are a function of church size and therefore also correlate with each other.

We found apostasy to show a significant relationship to the following variables:

1. Leadership style—As the pastor is more democratic and allows the members more voice in the operation of the church, apostasies go down.

2. New member involvement—As the church quickly involves new converts in the life and ministry of the congregation rather than ignoring them, apostasies tend to drop.

3. Atmosphere—Where the members rate climate in a

church as warm and friendly, apostasies decrease.

4. Devotions—In churches where a higher proportion of the membership has daily personal Bible study, we find fewer apostasies.

' 5. Standards—Where members perceive their church as holding high Adventist standards, usually we do not observe as many apostasies.

The findings on apostasy were particularly dramatic in our study of the churches in the Oregon Conference.[2] Here apostasies correlated − .470 with the actual growth rates and − .517 with the kingdom growth rates. We concluded that controlling the problem appears to be the most important single factor in promoting church growth in Oregon. You may also find this to be true in your congregation.

Approaching the Inactive

So apostasy is bad! What do we do about it? One thing might be to study inactive Adventists in your community. We need to listen to them—to find out what makes them tick. Only as we discover how we have failed such individuals in the past will we know how to protect God's flock in the future.

This calls for us to visit them in the spirit of humility, with the attitude of a learner, and with great sensitivity. Visits take time and patience, but in no other way will we really understand this large and neglected group among us. To aid in such contacts, the Institute of Church Ministry has developed the Former-Adventist Interview Schedule, an instrument pilot tested, used in studies in several conferences, and carefully revised. We show a copy of it on the following pages.

FORMER-ADVENTIST INTERVIEW SCHEDULE

(alternate wording for current members given in parentheses)

1. What was your <u>very first</u> contact with the Seventh-day Adventist Church?

   01 I was raised a Seventh-day Adventist
   02 Relative
   03 Adventist friend
   04 Series of evangelistic meetings
   05 Adventist radio or TV program
   06 Musical group
   07 Literature evangelist
   08 Health ministries
   09 Adventist books
   10 Adventist schools
   11 Request cards for literature
   12 Adventist spouse
   Other_____

2. Before you became a Seventh-day Adventist church member, what was your religious background?

   1 No religious background
   2 I was raised a Seventh-day Adventist
   3 Protestant (please specify denomination)_____
   4 Catholic
   Other_____

3. Would you mind telling me the factor which <u>most</u> attracted you to the Adventist message?

   1 I was raised an Adventist
   2 The truth and beauty of the Church's beliefs
   3 The warm fellowship I found among its believers
   4 The charisma of the minister/evangelist
   Other_____

4. Thinking back to the time <u>before</u> you became an Adventist, was there <u>one</u> thing that happened in your life which <u>especially</u> caused you to think about spiritual matters?

   00 Nothing
   01 Death of a friend or relative
   02 Divorce or marital problems
   03 Severe financial difficulties
   04 Retirement
   05 Began serious Bible study
   06 Concern for welfare of children
   07 Family problems (<u>not</u> including spouse)
   08 Marriage
   09 Witness of another person's changed life
   10 Dream or vision
   11 Life-threatening experience or illness
   12 Entrance into adulthood or other developmental stage
   13 Emptiness and dissatisfaction
   14 World conditions
   15 Adventist schools
   16 Loss of job
   17 Moved
   18 Personal emotional crisis
   Other_____

Institute of Church Ministry, 1982

5. If you were a student within the Seventh-day Adventist school system, please tell me the number of years you attended on each level.

I never attended Adventist schools_____
Elementary (grades 1-8)_____
Academy (grades 9-12) _____
College/university_____

6. How would you describe the kind of instruction you received before joining the Adventist Church?

1 Very thorough (more than I had expected)
2 Thorough (enough to prevent any "surprises")
3 Satisfactory (just enough to answer my questions)
4 Inadequate (I felt the instructor was rushing me. There were some surprises)
5 Very inadequate (I felt deceived)

7. How long did you study and evaluate the teachings of the Adventist Church before you became a member?

1 Can't say, was raised an Adventist
2 Less than 2 months
3 3 to 11 months
4 1 to 3 years
5 More than 3 years

8. On a scale of 1 to 5, at the time when you were most fully committed to the church, how would you rate your:

Witnessing in daily activities?   1 2 3 4 5
                                    Never   All the time

Church attendance?   1 2 3 4 5
                                    Irregular   Regular

Involvement in church life?   1 2 3 4 5
                                    None   Active

9. What kind of fellowship did you find in the Adventist Church?
                                    (have you found)

For example: Would you say the atmosphere was warm or cold? Did you feel comfortable with them? Did you make some Adventist friends?

_____

_____

10. For what length of time did you remain a member?
                                    (have you been)

1 Under 1 year   4 11-20 years
2 1-5 years   5 21 years or more
3 6-10 years

11. On a scale of 1 to 5, 1 being weak and 5 meaning strong, how important was
    each of the following factors in your decision to leave the church?
                                                          (stop attending)
    Weak   Strong
     1   2   3   4   5   Mistreated by members
     1   2   3   4   5   Social pressure from non-Adventist friends or relatives
     1   2   3   4   5   Lack of fellowship
     1   2   3   4   5   Don't believe some of the church's teachings? Which?

     1   2   3   4   5   Standards too strict
     1   2   3   4   5   Church's teaching and practice do not match
     1   2   3   4   5   Worship and program don't meet my spiritual needs

12. Did you have any of these feelings at the time you left the Adventist Church?
                                                          (stopped attending)

    Yes   No   Yes   No
     1   2   Bitterness   1   2   Confusion/ambivalence
     1   2   Guilt   1   2   Rebellion
     1   2   Relief   1   2   Hurt
     1   2   Sorrow   1   2   Emptiness
     1   2   Frustration   1   2   Indifference/boredom

13a. Other than a change in church   Things that happened:
     attendance, what is the first   00 Nothing
     thing or event that happened   01 Death of a friend or relative
     which began to move you away   02 Divorce or marital problems
     from a close tie to the church?   03 Drastic financial changes
     (From the list on the right,   04 Questioned church doctrine (s)
     place the number of the   05 Personal spiritual life
     event described in the blank.   a._____   declined (e.g. poor devotions)
     Use Other only if necessary)   06 Dissatisfaction with church's
     Other_____   programs
                                          07 Birth/adoption of a child
     _____   08 Marriage
                                          09 Conflicts with Sabbath-keeping
     _____   10 Problems keeping church standards
                                              (e.g. health, tithing, dress)
  b. Describe what happened next.   11 Personal or family illness
     (Place the number of this   12 Entered new developmental stage
     next item in the blank.   b._____ 13 Influenced by parents
     Remember, use Other only if   14 Influenced by children
     necessary)   15 Influenced by a relative
     Other)_____   16 Influenced by non-SDA friends
                                          17 Moved
     _____   18 Unpleasant experience with
                                              church member (s)
     _____   19 Unpleasant experience with
                                              a pastor
  c. Please tell me what finally   20 No church fellowship or support
     led you to break from the   in my personal crisis
     church.   21 Became involved with another
     (Place the number of the event   denomination
     in the blank)   c._____
     Other_____

     _____

it
r
rrent
mbers)

14. Was it your decision to withdraw your membership from the church or was your name dropped without your consent?

    0 Question not applicable
    1 My decision
    2 Church's decision with my consent and agreement
    3 Church's decision without my consent and agreement
    4 I was not even consulted

15. What effort did the church make to reclaim you between the time you stopped attending and the time your name was actually removed from the membership list? (What effort has the church made to bring you back into full fellowship?)

Yes	No	
1	2	Pastoral visit
1	2	Member visit
1	2	Literature or letters
1	2	Phone calls

nit
or
rrent
mbers)

16. Did you join a church of another denomination?   Yes___ No___
    If so, which one?_____

17. Please state briefly the main thing that could have been different and would have encouraged you in your experience with the Adventist Church?_____
    _____

nit
or
urrent
embers)

18. What are the chances that you might again become a Seventh-day Adventist someday?

    1 Very likely
    2 Likely
    3 Don't know
    4 Unlikely
    5 Very unlikely

19. Is there anything that stands in the way of your return to membership in the church?_____   (active participation in)
    _____

20. How would you describe your present personal relationship with Jesus Christ?
    _____

21. Your sex:
             ____Male   ____ Female

22. Your age group:
                    ____19 or under   ____36-50 years
                    ____20-35 years   ____51-65 years   ____65 or over

Additional comments: _____
_____

You will have two classes of people to contact and interview:

1. Those whose names a congregation has dropped from its records for reason of apostasy.

2. Those who are still officially members but who have not been attending.

We offer the following as suggested approaches for gaining the cooperation of each category. *Suggested procedure to those dropped from fellowship:*

Good morning. I'm _____ from the Adventist Church [if the person doesn't know you]. I've come to ask a favor of you.

[Here he/she may invite you in or at least ask, "What is it?"]

As a church we have become aware of the necessity of becoming more sensitive to the needs of our members and others whom we serve. We would like very much to do a better job. To do this we need to know what we may be doing wrong and what we could be doing better. So we are asking members and former members to help us. I understand that you used to be a member of our church. Therefore, you have a perspective on what is happening that we don't have. Your viewpoint is very valuable to us. Would you mind taking just a few minutes to talk with me about your experience with the church? I'd like to ask several questions and jot down some of your major observations.

[If there is some resistance, continue with the following:]

I haven't come to blame you or criticize you or pressure you in any way. I've come only to ask you for help. What you can teach us may mean that other people in the future will have a better experience with the church.

Suggested approach to those not attending but still members:

Good morning. I'm _____ from the Adventist Church [if the person doesn't know you]. I've come to ask a favor of you.

[Here he/she may invite you in or at least ask, "What is it?"]

As a church, we have become aware of the necessity of becoming more sensitive to the needs of our members and others whom we serve. We would like very much to do a better job. To do this we need to know what we may be doing wrong and what we could be doing better. So we are asking members and former members to help us.

You are a member of the church, but we've missed you lately. Apparently you don't feel about the church the same as you once did. Since you look at the church from a little different perspective than I do, your viewpoint is very valuable to me and to the church. Would you mind taking just a few minutes to talk about your experience? I'd like to ask several questions and jot down some of your major observations.

[If you sense some resistance, continue with:]

I haven't come to blame you or criticize you or pressure you in any way. I've come to ask you for help. What you can teach us may mean that other people in the future will have a better experience with the church.

We do not intend these approaches to be rigid and exact. You do not need to memorize them. They just indicate the general manner in which the interviews should proceed. Become familiar with them and then put the ideas and concepts into your own words. Different people under different circumstances will require other approaches. The most important thing is to be warm, friendly, and accepting.

When the person you are calling on is still officially a member but not attending, omit questions 14, 16, and 18, and slightly restructure questions 9, 10, 11, 12, 15, and 19 (alternate wording is given in parentheses). Questions 21 and 22 should not be asked but should be filled in by the interviewer.

The order of the questions follows a logical flow in discussing the experience of the member. The interview starts in a spiritual, yet nonthreatening, way and then moves into some of the deeper areas. Yet the visitor should be flexible. If a member begins to talk about areas not yet reached on the schedule, allow him or her to do so. Make notes and come back to skipped material later.

The visitor does not give the schedule to the former member. He should keep it in a binder or clipboard, and as the conversation proceeds, he should mark answers or write in information in brief form. It may be best for the two to sit side by side so that the former member can see what the visitor is writing. The situation must determine exact procedure. The former member's name does not appear on the questionnaire, and the interviewer should assure him or her that the information is confidential. But check the name off the master list after the interview.

The attitude of the visitor is the most vital element in the success of the study. The church often considers ex-members traitors or enemies. Some practical rules that will ensure success are:

1. A vital aspect is the manner in which the church representative approaches the ex-member. Normally when a backslider faces a minister or a member of the church, he either locks himself up or adopts an attitude of attack or self-defense. Such postures are perfectly understandable in the light of his previous unpleasant experiences with the church.

Remember that the main motive of this particular visit is not to convince him or her to return to the fellowship, but rather to secure information and advice to help improve the life of the congregation. The goal is to search for possible harmful elements that we could eliminate to avoid future mistakes. The church is *eager* to listen. Make this clear at the very beginning in order to create an open and relaxed atmosphere. Of course, if the Spirit should work upon the heart of the former member in such a way as to cause him or her to be receptive to an invitation, the visitor must be prepared to follow His leading. Sensitivity is essential here.

2. The selection of the visitor is vital. It would be ideal if a minister not involved with the life of that congregation, and therefore neutral to the particular situations mentioned, could be the visiting pastor. This is especially true when visible problems exist in the church—such as ethnic, social, or family divisions among members. Church members clearly identified with one side of a church conflict *should not* visit ex-members, because it obviously would close the door to an open interaction. Lay leaders who are open, caring persons and who have special training for this work may make good visitors.

3. Ask the questions in the most natural way possible, avoiding any semblance of a cross-examination.

4. Make the visit by appointment. This will avoid unnecessary pressure and will create a more relaxed environment.

5. Receive and accept all the observations by the ex-member without defense or justification. The visitor needs to know the facts—the evaluation will come later. Sometimes the former member will make strong accusations against the

ministry, the denomination, or the local leadership of the church. Do not react defensively, but jot down every observation or idea, encouraging the person to talk freely. It is relatively easy to discover whether the person is bitter and frustrated or speaking objectively.

6. Try to assess whether the ex-member's real reasons for dropping out resulted from doctrinal problems or interpersonal relationships.

7. Be sincerely thankful for every idea expressed and promise to take them to the church to study as the members search for ways in which they may improve.

Offer support without manipulation as the Holy Spirit guides. Since the visitor is a Christian ambassador and not simply a researcher, he/she will be ready to seize the divine opportunity if it comes. Items 19 and 20 may introduce it.

Fordyce Detamore, a specialist in this area, suggested several "do's" for those working with backsliders. His principles, listed below, may be wisely applied to the visitation program described above:

1. Come to the point quickly. It shortens the period of dread and discomfort natural in such a situation.

2. Let the bitterness come out. The former member will probably "unload his pent-up hatred." Listen kindly and interestedly.

3. Don't defend anyone. Rallying to the aid of an "enemy" of the backslider identifies yourself as an "enemy" also.

4. Don't betray the backslider's confidence by telling others what should be kept secret.

5. Don't make the visit long. In that way you leave the door open for another contact.

6. Always close with prayer.

In several places where individuals have tried this method, inactive members have returned to the fellowship of the church. But this is in addition to the fact that the primary purpose of the visit was to *listen* to former members, to learn from them, and to use those discoveries in shaping the future behavior of the church. The very act of being listened to in a sympathetic manner, however, may break the ice of hostility and cause warm memories to surface. Always remember—

your visit may be the bridge across which the former member may find his or her way back to the church. The Caring Church is just as interested in those who have drifted away as in those who have never heard the gospel.

What Former Adventists Say

Using the interview schedule, visitors called on 120 former or inactive Adventists in the Upper Columbia Conference in 1980 and 1981. A summary of their findings will illustrate the kinds of information that the method can produce:

The religious background former members most frequently indicated was the Adventist Church. Almost one out of every two persons had been raised Adventist (46 percent). About 26 percent came from other Protestant faiths before joining our denomination. Besides Adventist upbringing, those contacted frequently cited some kind of personal relationship with an Adventist member as their point of contact. As a whole, former members reported minimal attendance at Adventist schools, only 28 percent having completed eight years of Adventist education.

No one reason adequately describes what attracted former members to the church in the first place. Half did not mention any specific crisis or event that stimulated interest in spiritual matters. The large percentage of those who had an Adventist upbringing suggests many naturally and uneventfully grew into church membership. The largest single group, 24 percent, indicated the truth of the church's teachings attracted them the most. The witness of members' lives and the charisma of the pastor or evangelist also sparked interest in Adventism.

Former members' experiences in the church exhibit certain traits. About two thirds (67 percent) felt their prebaptismal instruction to have been thorough or very thorough. Another 18 percent regarded the instruction adequate. Apart from those who mentioned their Adventist background (37 percent), 31 percent studied the church's teachings from three to eleven months. About 16 percent spent less than two months examining Adventist beliefs. They generally considered their baptismal instruction good in

146

terms of depth and length of time of study. However, once in
the church, some 63 percent became only nominally involved.
They participated in the church only through either regular
or irregular worship attendance. Also, whereas 48 percent
reported a warm fellowship in the congregation, another 48
percent felt different degrees of discomfort with other
members. Generally speaking, former members were not
fully involved in the local church's programs and ministries
and were divided in their descriptions of the church's
fellowship atmosphere.

Some significant characteristics of the process of leaving
the church emerge from the responses. Twenty-eight percent
of the former members spent one to five years in the church.
Of the 30 percent that spoke about the actual decision to leave,
the majority personally withdrew their membership or agreed
with the church's action. A lack of fellowship was the strongest
factor influencing personal decisions to leave (24 percent).
Dissatisfaction with the church's worship and programs and
the influence of non-Adventist friends or relatives also had
significant impact on the choice to break with it. Former
members experienced frustration, relief, and bitterness
during the process of leaving. Coupled with the former
members' part in withdrawing their membership, these
feelings may indicate a willingness to depart. Put simply, they
were glad to go. An unpleasant experience with the members
or the pastor was the most frequently cited event or change
that moved individuals away from the denomination. Other
changes mentioned include dissatisfaction with the church's
programs, personal failure to keep church standards or
teachings, marital or family problems, and the influence of
other persons. The congregation did little to reclaim such
persons *before* they lost their membership. Only half said the
pastor visited them. Even fewer mentioned that a church
member had come to see them (34 percent). Few church
members or leaders cared enough to try to stop them.

Those surveyed manifested a variety of post-membership
attitudes. Very few had joined another denomination after
leaving the Adventist Church. Of those who did respond to
the question about what could have been different in their

experience with the church, nearly all gave answers suggesting more loving, consistent, and supportive relationships with other members. Former members appeared mainly undecided or pessimistic about the chances of their ever becoming Adventists again. Only 10 percent expressed any hope of joining once more. When asked what obstacle currently blocked renewed membership, about 43 percent indicated that no real obstructions existed except possibly their having no desire to return. Some former members also counted their current life style as incompatible with church teachings. Their present relationship with Christ varied considerably. Roughly 47 percent depicted their spiritual experiences as either very good or, at least, growing. Another 37 percent said their relationship with the Lord was either very weak or nonexistent.

The majority of those who left the church were female. Nearly half the former members fall into the 20-to-35-years-of-age bracket. When compared with the other age groups, this figure is alarmingly high.

The Save

If stemming the flow of discouraged and disgruntled members from the church is such a vital part of a growth strategy, then it calls for creative methods to deal with the problem. One helpful approach might be to broaden our system of pastoral recognition to include the prevention of apostasy. The sports world long judged baseball pitchers by such statistics as games won and earned run averages. But with the development of the relief pitcher as a specialist came the need for a new category—the save. He steps in when the starter is beginning to falter but while his team is still ahead. If he can prevent the game from being lost, he is credited with a save.

Now in the pastoral ministry, the conferences keep a record of new converts and credit each minister with the number. But if a pastor brings back an erring sheep who has not actually been dropped from membership and therefore cannot be counted as a baptism, he or she has no way to report the fact. Since it is a law of human behavior that we tend to do that for which we receive rewards, the minister with a multitude of pressing duties may find it easy to neglect the wandering ones.

But the prevention of an apostasy is as important to church growth as the baptism of a new convert. As has the sports world, we may need to institute the category of "saves." A pastor could have a place to report those members who had ceased regular attendance and an Adventist life style, but who had been restored to active membership through his or her ministry.

Another approach the Caring Church may use is the spiritual guardian or "buddy" system. Every member is responsible for some other member. The small group system can include several inactive members in each fellowship group where they become the special targets of love and concern. George Knowles even recommends giving former members territorial assignments as a means of rekindling their love for Christ.[3]

Church growth, both spiritual and numerical, moves forward when we control and eliminate apostasy. We can best accomplish this by fostering the spiritual life of the members, actively involving them in the internal and outreach life of the church, and creating a climate that is warm, friendly, and caring.

References
[1] Dudley and Cummings, "Church Growth in the North American Division," pp. 35-38, 81-86, 94, 95, 113-117, 131-133.
[2] Dudley, Cummings, and Ritterskamp, "Church Growth in the Oregon Conference," pp. 37, 38.
[3] Knowles, *How to Help Your Church Grow*, pp. 95-97.

13

The Church's Agenda in the Coming Decade

In view of all that we have presented, what kind of priorities should church leadership set for the years just ahead? We believe there are several important considerations.

Biblical Priorities

The future of Seventh-day Adventist Church growth is dependent primarily upon our willingness to let the priorities of Scripture guide us. We should give great attention to the book of Acts as the record of God's principles of church growth. To the extent that Seventh-day Adventists order their lives, organizations, and policies by those principles, we will realize the blessing of the Holy Spirit. The power of prayer, fellowship, worship, and witness must center in and be dependent upon Jesus Christ and His Spirit. It is the greatest need of the church today and in the decade to come.

Pastor Support System

Pastors would welcome a support system that they would count on for viable answers to issues faced by the local congregation. Issues such as specific problems in church

151

discipline, family life, youth ministry, church finance, cultural challenges to Christian faith, pastoral nurture, and reaching the unchurched. The local conference level could provide the system if the pastor could be assured that a group of experts will be "on call" to provide the information and resources needed for church growth. It would greatly enhance the pastor's sense of security, peace of mind, and morale.

Evangelistic Research and Development

The present cost of public evangelism demands that the church give careful study to improving its effectiveness. Several evangelists are already utilizing research techniques to evaluate and enhance their methods. It is vital that we examine the types of people the church reaches through all its evangelistic methods, and then we must develop new approaches for categories that the present techniques do not touch. Evangelism will not become outdated if updated through research.

Witness Training

Research on the Seventh-day Adventist member reveals that he or she is quite involved in life-style witnessing, giving Bible studies, and community service. However, most members feel the need for instruction in how to witness. Many church members seek skills in practical relation building and natural sharing of Scripture truth in a variety of settings. This calls for a relational versus informational form of training. Adventists desire a witness life style. As leaders, we must provide that which will help them realize their goal. From the pastor's perspective, activating members is his or her greatest frustration. We must give careful study to educating the ministry in motivation and training skills.

Youth Ministry

This decade will witness a great increase in second-, third-, and fourth-generation Seventh-day Adventists. The issues faced by many local congregations will revolve around attracting, activating, and holding youth. Church growth will depend in large measure on our effectiveness in revitalizing older congregations with young enthusiastic Christians.

Education

-While education in the future will encounter even more financial pressures, the greatest issues it struggles with may be of a philosophical nature. Religious education must focus on assisting youth to actualize their faith, resulting in the ability to live in the world but not of it. If religious education does not distinguish itself by providing students with a sense of mission and meaning, it will lose its reason for existence.

Decision Support System

Informed decisions are wise decisions. Present administrators find their leadership hampered by their lack of information. A decision support system would provide them with a forecast of church growth trends in their conferences. Such predictions would point out potential problem areas, thus allowing leaders to act on a problem before it becomes a crisis. This is known as proactive leadership, as opposed to reactive leadership, which responds only to crises. Present reporting systems do not deliver such data to the administrator; thus, the church at large is jeopardized.

Time Management

Assertions of commitment to church growth have a hollow ring unless the time of leaders, agendas of committees, and management of resources verify the verbiage. One of the most serious problems facing all levels of ministry is time management. A conference president or church pastor can ill afford to be absent from his area of service. Yet we find that the average pastor spends 58.8 days per year traveling, 43 days at camp meetings and on vacation, and 34 days in weekly time-off activities. We would not eliminate travel, vacation, days off, or camp meetings, but only remind the pastor that before he makes a visit, or studies for a session, or holds a committee, he or she has already spent 37 percent of the year in the activities listed above. It only highlights the fact that poor time management or misplaced priorities will render him or her ineffective.

We would imagine that a study of a president's time would reveal that he is all too often out of his area of service, thus limiting his effectiveness. Relationship is the vehicle for spiritual growth, and the prerequisite of relationship building is time. If we want to build deep relationships with people, we must allocate significant portions of time on a regular basis to them.

Quick encounters will ensure superficial relationships with minimal long-term spiritual impact. Thus short pastoral tenure combined with limited time for establishing relationships with the unchurched severely limits church growth. Administrators and pastors must give careful study to arranging their priorities in such a way that they spend at least an equal amount of time leading the church in ministry to the nonmember as to the member. Committees must put first priority on mission strategies, as opposed to institutional maintenance. In short, from the local church to the General Conference, each segment must on a personal and corporate level place prime valve on time devoted to mission.

Need-focused Ministry

Talking about the building of relationships leads us to reemphasize a major theme of this book: The church must gear its ministry to the felt needs of the communities that surround local congregations. The most exciting concept of recent years is the Caring Church model—a redemptive community that focuses on people and their needs.

One of the authors recalls his early days in the pastoral ministry. He emerged from college with a mistaken idea of why people join the church. "Convince them that the Bible supports the doctrines of the Seventh-day Adventist Church," he assumed, "and they will have no other recourse than to enter the baptismal waters."

So he sallied forth, armed with proof texts, and found that indeed he could best most of the non-Adventists he encountered. They could not match his logical reasoning and superior firepower. But he soon discovered that they did have other recourses than accepting his faith and uniting with his church. They could (and did) lock their doors when he called and avoid him like the plague. Converts were few in his early ministry.

Gradually the truth dawned. People do not join churches simply because of teachings that are true and Biblical. Few humans make any kind of life-style change solely on the intellectual basis of true or false, right or wrong. People change because the proposed action promises to offer them something personal in the form of more effective living.

Modern behavioral science has helped us to see that people are motivated to do that which will bring need satisfaction. All of us are created with intrinsic needs—physical, psychological, and emotional. The need to feel safe, to love and be loved, the need for self-esteem and the esteem of others, to do something significant with our lives, is a part of each one of us. And while many frantically try to meet these needs in self-destructive and unfulfilling ways, yet the needs themselves are legitimate. God placed them in the human breast, and only He knows how to satisfy them in ways that enhance human dignity. One of our favorite texts is: "My God will meet all your needs according to his glorious riches in Christ Jesus" (Phil. 4:19).

How does God take care of these needs? Often through the church. We become God's co-workers to supply the deep, heartfelt longings of our fellow humans. This is what the Caring Church is all about. The church that would grow must become the church that serves. The Caring Church is not another program conceived at hierarchical levels far from the grass roots and imposed on unwilling pastors and members. It is an attitude, a way of life, a redemptive community. It stops talking at people and listens to them. It starts with what *they* think they need instead of what *we* think they need. It makes convincing them secondary to loving them.

As members, pastors, and administrators catch this vision, they will see that church growth is not an imposed burden or a "numbers game." It will increasingly become an exciting adventure with God.